HIGHER VI...

VIBRATIONAL HEALING FOR AN EMPOWERED LIFE

By Karen Frazier

Cover photography by Jayme Tomasek

Cover design by Karen Frazier

ISBN-13: 978-0692896259 (Afterlife Publishing)

ISBN-10: 0692896252

For Paul, a spirit guide with a sense of humor and a sometimes pushy attitude

Introduction – Vibin'

I am a vibrational healer, or at least that's part of what I do. I call myself an intuitive energy healer. When I say that to people, some tend to look at me funny while others nod sagely, as if to say, *Ah yes*. Still, I'd guess that aside from those sages with the knowing smiles, many people have no clue what intuitive energy healer or vibrational healer means. There are so many uses of terms like vibrational or energy healing, it could mean almost anything.

What I mean when I say this is I work with energy frequencies (vibrations) that affect the body, mind, and spirit, and I attempt to help people change those vibrations so they can heal themselves. So while for the sake of pithy labeling, my bio says, *Karen Frazier is an intuitive energy healer*, what it really should say (but it's just too darn wordy) is, *Karen Frazier offers modalities to help others adjust their personal energy frequencies (vibrations) to a vibe that is beneficial so they can discover their own means of healing for body, mind, and spirit.*

In other words, I'm not the healer. You are.

Each of us only has the power to heal one person, and that's ourselves. It doesn't matter if you're a doctor, nurse, chiropractor, massage therapist, Reiki master, faith healer, or anything else. You cannot cause someone else's healing. Only they can do that for themselves. One can, however, help someone discover what needs healing and find ways to work on it. In a nutshell, that's what I do. The healing doesn't come from me unless I'm trying to heal myself. It comes from you, and everyone has the capacity to bring about their own healing if they so choose and it serves their highest and greatest good.

What Is Healing, Anyway?

Healing is another nebulous term that means different things to different people. For some, it may mean the cessation of uncomfortable physical symptoms. For others, it may mean forgiveness of self or another. Some may see it as a communion with spirit. Some may see it as obtaining balance in body, mind, and spirit. I think it is all of these things and more.

However, for the purposes of this book, I will define healing as, *clearing blockages of body, mind, and spirit that do not serve one's greatest and highest good,* and *raising one's vibrational energy to the highest level possible in order to raise the vibration of the planet.*

Greatest and Highest Good

You'll see me use the phrase *highest and greatest good* frequently. The phrase can be subjective, but I'll attempt to define it.

I believe we are all spiritual beings; that is, we are pieces of the Source (the Divine, or whatever else you want to call it) who choose to come live as embodied humans on the planet Earth. Before we come, we make plans for this lifetime, such as lessons we'd like to learn or things we'd like to accomplish (the *karmic imprint* we bring into our embodied life). Then we're born, and we forget who we truly are, why we came, and what we came here to do. We become absorbed in the illusion.

As we go through life, our higher selves (souls) provide opportunities for our embodied selves to do the things we set out to accomplish. However, as beings of free will, we can choose to seize these opportunities, or we can do something else altogether. It's entirely up to us and because we don't remember who we truly are, we often make choices that are different than the path our higher selves have chosen for us. When that happens, we may slip out of balance because we are not serving our highest purpose. In other words, we are not serving our highest and greatest good.

It's virtually impossible from an embodied state to define exactly what our highest and greatest good is because from the perspective of our limited human minds, we may not even be able to conceive of the grand plans our Divine selves have for us. So what serves your greatest and highest good may not be what you think it is because your higher self may have something even cooler planned for you than you could ever imagine.

Your Divine Guidance System

We do, however, have a *Divine guidance system* that can help us to make choices that move us in the direction of our greatest and highest good. This guidance system has many members from nonphysical realms including your spirit guides who walk with you along your life's path, your higher self, loved ones who have passed before you and watch over you, your own wisdom you've collected from your past incarnations that exist within your Akash, higher beings of Light who choose to communicate, and many others.

You receive messages from your Divine guidance system via a combination of intuition (everybody has it), emotions (whether you feel peace or agitation, love or fear, etc.), experiences (whether you're doing something you love or hate, etc.), your dreams, and how your body feels. Your Divine guidance system may also cause small energetic flares of recognition when you come to a point on your path that is particularly important or when you make a choice that resonates with your soul's guidance. It's like an energetic fist pump, and it may occur in many ways, such as a feeling of instant recognition when you meet someone, a sense of déjà vu, a significant dream, a compulsion to do something you wouldn't normally consider doing, etc. You still have the free will to ignore this guidance, and you also have the ability to ask for the guidance when you feel you need help.

The Universal Two-by-Four

When we choose to move away from our greatest and highest good, as we have free will to do, our Divine guidance system seeks to get our attention, and one way to do it is through our bodies. It may start gently with a little ache or pain here or there but if we continue to move in a direction that doesn't serve us, Spirit may become a bit more insistent, and symptoms or illnesses may worsen as a way to show us we are out of balance.

This doesn't just happen in our bodies, however. It can happen in other aspects of our lives, as well. When we are out of balance and not moving in a direction that serves our greatest and highest good, we may notice it in our relationships, jobs, finances, or elsewhere. For instance, drama may erupt in our lives. We may have trouble sleeping. We may feel angry, bitter, or restless.

When we are not in harmony with our greatest and highest good, our Divine guidance system does what it can to get our attention. What may start as small incidents can grow broader and more obvious until finally we get what I fondly refer to as the *universal two-by-four*; a figurative two-by-four

10

slaps us violently upside the head. Depending on the system it affects, this two-by-four manifests in many different ways. For instance, it could appear as the loss of a job, the end of a relationship, major financial difficulties, the loss of your home, or a debilitating illness. When these things occur, we have no choice but to pay attention and make adjustments.

Responsibility, Not Blame

I feel it's tricky to discuss the universal two-by-four because inevitably someone asks, "Does that mean I am to blame for (fill in the blank)?"

My response is this: "It's not a matter of blame."

Responsibility and blame are not the same thing. Blame is judgmental and reactive, while taking responsibility is non-judgmental and proactive. Blame implies someone has done something wrong and is at fault, while accepting responsibility implies you accept how your choices or actions brought about current circumstances and indicates willingness to change those choices or actions in order to bring about a change of circumstances or experience.

I am a firm believer every person does the very best they can given what they know and understand, the filters through which they see the world, and the tools they have to work with. When they know differently, understand more, and have more effective tools, they make choices that are more in line with what best serves them.

As souls in human bodies, we've forgotten a lot. We don't have all of the truths of our ultimate reality in our conscious minds, and we therefore sometimes (often) make choices that are quite different than we would if we came into our bodies with our full soul knowledge. We believe we are at the mercy of outside forces, lack control of the thoughts that arise in our minds, and our words and actions arising from those outside forces and thoughts are a justified reaction we have no choice but to make. Most of us for most of our lives have no clue we can choose what we think and say in response to what appears to be outside stimulus. We also don't realize the outside stimulus are actually events we've conspired with our higher selves to create in our lives.

So, while we do bear responsibility for the state of our lives, relationships, and health because of our thoughts, words, and deeds, as well as the challenges and opportunities we set up for ourselves before we came into this incarnation, we are not to blame because by design, we lack a clear understanding of just how this universal stuff works. However, we do still bear responsibility for everything in our lives and once we acknowledge that responsibility, we can begin to make choices to help us heal.

Chronic Conditions

Sometimes in spite of all of the work you're doing on your spiritual path, chronic conditions may flare and become symptomatic. While these may be part of old energy still working its way from your body to make new energy, it can also help you to realize there are deeper seated issues that could still use a little loving.

In my personal experience, I've found self-love and self-awareness happen in layers. The issues I am most likely to recognize and work on are those that are the closest to the surface because they are the easiest to notice and typically make the most "noise." When I peel away those layers through the process of vibrational healing and self love, it exposes new ones that were safely ensconced beneath the surface.

As embodied humans, we are deeply complex that way. From the moment of our birth, when we are born forgetting who we truly our, the circumstances of our embodied lives pile on layer after layer of beliefs, societal norms, and things that hurt us, mold us, and shape us into who we become as adults. Our self-image is filled with misperceptions, buried pain, and beliefs about ourselves, others, and the benevolence (or lack thereof) of life that helps us maintain the illusion of separation from the whole. Add these to the original gifts we gave ourselves before we even arrived in this embodied lifetime, such as circumstances, health conditions, and traits designed to help us work on our own spiritual evolution, as well as any karmic issues we may be carrying from past incarnations, and it begins to grow clear just how complex of a puzzle each embodied human actually is.

Chronic conditions, then, give you repeated opportunities to peel away another layer, and another, and another. While they don't feel like a gift in the moment (and trust me, I know and understand this well – I have three chronic conditions: celiac disease, Hashimoto's thyroiditis, and a severe dairy allergy), chronic conditions are like old friends coming to help you peel away another layer. They provide an opportunity to uncover and release more about yourself.

For example, just last fall I had a flare of my Hashimoto's thyroiditis, which is a chronic, autoimmune condition. For the most part, I am able to control it through diet, exercise, and a small amount of natural desiccated thyroid medication, but occasionally I experience a flare anyway, usually caused by some type of stressor in my life that results in additional inflammation.

The flare started after several months of stress I was choosing not to acknowledge. I had a longtime friendship end in what I felt at the time was a nasty betrayal. Instead of just ending the friendship and walking away, the other person then decided to talk about me behind my back, engage in some bullying tactics, and even attempted to steal money from me via an account for which (s)he had somehow discovered the password. I decided to "take the high road" and attempted to ignore this other person, not reciprocate the negative talk, and not give the behaviors any outward attention.

On the inside, however, I was upset. I was hurt and confused. I was worried others were going to believe the trash talk. While my public persona said, *Nothing to see here, just move along*, inside I was definitely not ignoring it. In other words, my public reaction was inauthentic, although I was unaware that was the case.

In the midst of this, my beloved nephew accidentally conked me on the head with a car door, which caused a concussion. This appeared to be the final stressor, and suddenly I was in a full-blown flare of my autoimmune condition. Fortunately, the concussion provided me with plenty of time to just be. Concussion protocols dictate not doing anything with your body or brain until the fog and symptoms lift.

It took mine a few weeks. However, I discovered the two weeks were a gift. While I sat around twiddling my thumbs and healing, I recognized another layer of my own bullshit coming back at me in how I reacted to this lost friendship and the subsequent cold war that followed. It occurred to me during that time my reactions to the other person's behaviors had nothing to do with him/her and everything to do with me. You'd think I would have discovered this a long time ago, but our belief in our humanity and duality is deeply ingrained. Once I got past the dismay (and self-judgment) of realizing I'd done everything to myself and was the cause of my own pain, I was able to see old patterns of self-blame and fears about being unlovable coming to the surface and manifesting as my old friend and teacher, Hashimoto's disease. And then I was able to apply the vibrational healing tools I had at my disposal to truly heal. My former friend gave me the gift of self-recognition, self-awareness, and healing.

So if you have a chronic condition and it flares up from time to time, return to your tools. Take a look at your thoughts and beliefs and see what might still need healing. As long as we are embodied as humans, we will have this work to do. It is the work of Spirit, and each layer we peel away moves us closer to true enlightenment. Instead of self-judgment and self-blame, when you experience a flare, recognize it for the gift it is and love it so you can heal the next layer.

How Is Dysfunction Serving You?

Often when we experience some type of chronic dysfunction whether emotional, physical, mental, or spiritual, although we tell ourselves we don't like it, when we dig deeper with integrity and emotional honesty, we discover the dysfunction is serving some purpose in our lives.

Here's an example. I struggled for many years with morbid obesity and chronic pain issues. Every day, I was in moderate to severe pain that limited my mobility, exhausted me, and left me feeling generally terrible. Because of that, I was often unable to do much around the house. Many days, it took all my energy to get out of bed, do my job, and care for my children. On the days I felt better, I could also move a little more and do some extra housework. Several years ago, I decided it was time to start working with the obesity and pain because I was just tired of it.

As I explored energetically, I discovered many ways both the pain and obesity had been serving me all along:

- I believed I was the only one in the family who ever did any housework. Being ill and in severe pain provided me an excuse to demand someone else do the housework for me. Somehow, I felt I couldn't be in an authentic place and ask for help with my own voice. Instead, I used my pain to force my family into helping.
- In my early 20s when I was thin and attractive, I grew frustrated with being an object of desire to men. It felt as if nobody recognized my spirit, heart, or brain, and all they saw was my body. When I gained weight, I felt people were forced to get to know and love the real me, and it stopped the constant attention I received from men.
- I used to be a generally shy person who felt awkward interacting with people I didn't know. Being fat made me invisible so I had an excuse not to interact as much, and being in pain kept me at home or just hanging out with old friends instead of having to take the risk of meeting somebody new.
- Being fat gave me a built in excuse when somebody I met didn't like me. I could blame

it on my physique instead of looking at what I was projecting that was unlikeable.

- As an empath (I feel other people's emotions and pain as if they are my own), both the weight and the pain offered me a protective layer to block out the emotions and physical pain I received from others.

These were just a few of the many ways I discovered my health issues served me. If you'd asked me when I was in the depths of them, I would have told you I hated being fat and in pain, and it served no purpose. When I looked more deeply, however, I discovered it gave me a sense of power and control. It provided me an excuse to make things all about me and use it to exert control. It also allowed me to feel less accountable because I had a ready excuse.

When I realized just how poorly these things served me, I was able to take the steps that led to genuine and lasting change. As I worked with clearing the blockages and rebalancing energy, things changed. I lost almost 150 pounds. I started moving more. My pain faded and is virtually nonexistent now. However, I had to recognize how I was using those aspects of my health, and I had to have a genuine desire for change in order to remove them.

At first when I recognized this, I reacted with self-judgment. As the self-judgment faded, however, I was delighted I had learned something new about myself and excited about the realization I had the power to change if I truly wanted it.

So again, it's not about self-blame. It is, however, about self-responsibility. Everyone has issues and circumstances in his or her life they believe they don't want, but somewhere deep inside they are serving an ego-driven purpose. The first step is discovering those ego-driven purposes and deciding just how important they really are to you. Are they more important than living a vibrant and joyful life? If they are, that's okay. Just be aware of your true motivations and how they serve you. You are allowed to live within those motivations for as long as you choose and as long as you feel they serve you. However, if at some point you find they no longer serve you, know you can choose something else.

How do your current dysfunctions serve you? Do they keep you from feeling afraid, allow you a sense of control, or give you an excuse? When and if you are ready, ask yourself these questions and others as a precursor to releasing that which no longer serves your greatest and highest good.

Existing as Embodied Egos

Our Divine souls exist in a much different environment than we, as embodied humans, do. In a soul state, everything is love and light, there is no duality, and there's no such thing as judgment or fear. In our non-physical expression, we are one with everything and everyone; there is no separation.

However, when we are embodied, we don't exist in the same environment. We come into this world believing we are alone and experiencing ourselves as separate from everyone and everything else. We have something called ego that causes us to experience separation. We come into our bodies believing in the illusion of duality. We believe in our experiences of duality (darkness and light, love and fear, judgment and oneness, etc.) because the embodied human experience is, by design, immersive. It is designed that way so we can begin to work our way back towards enlightenment (oneness) in the context of the human experience.

Thought, Word, and Action

We are creative individuals. We create all of the circumstances and outcomes in our life through our thoughts, words, and actions. Masaru Emoto showed how the vibration of thoughts and words affect matter. In his book *Messages from Water,* Emoto shows images from the results of experiments he performed. He filled several containers with water. To each, he attached a piece of paper with a word printed on it. Some were positive words and phrases, such as love, compassion, or peace. Others were negative, such as *I hate you,* or, *You're ugly.*

After Emoto exposed the water to the phrases, he froze each sample and then photographed the water crystals. What he found was astounding. Those connected with negative words and phrases had indiscernible patterns, dark cloudiness, and appeared chaotic. Those exposed to the positive words and phrases, however, developed beautiful, complex, and ordered crystal patterns similar to what you'd see in snowflakes. It is a powerful illustration of how thoughts and words affect vibration.

In the vibrational healing classes I teach, I perform a similar demonstration. I fill two bags with small semiprecious gemstones (usually round beads or chips). I write *I love you,* on one card and *I hate you* on another and seal them both in an unlabeled envelope. Then I mix the envelopes up so I don't know which is which, and I put one in each bag and seal it. I leave it for a week and then bring the bags to my class. I give class participants one crystal from each bag and ask them to hold one in each hand to see if they can feel differences in the energy and guess which is from the *I love you* bag and which is from the *I hate you* bag. Class participants are remarkably accurate at feeling the difference between the two and correctly identifying which was exposed to each energy, which I reveal by opening each envelope in the class. It's a powerful illustration of how thoughts and words affect energy and vibration.

If thoughts and words have that much of an effect on crystals or on water, imagine how they affect the human body, which is about 60 percent water (and as high as 75 percent in the brain).

Creating Your Own Experience

Each of us, through how we think, what we say, and what we do, creates our own experience in this lifetime. However, most of us don't realize we are responsible for the things that appear in our lives. Therefore, if we don't like our circumstances, we can change them by creating something else.

It's a simple concept that is complex in execution because consciously controlling the creations that appear in your life involves consistent attention to your thoughts, judgments, fears, words, and actions. And with that constant attention needs to come the effort of also choosing different thoughts, words, judgments, and actions and releasing fear in order to move in the direction you believe you'd like to go.

Body, Mind, and Spirit Balance

Health isn't merely an absence of symptoms or disease. If I have a headache, I can take an aspirin and the symptoms may go away, but that doesn't mean I've cleared the underlying causes. It only means I've used an artificial method (something from outside of me – in this case a drug) to remove a symptom, but the underlying imbalance that caused it is still there. If I have a diseased organ, doctors can remove it from my body, but that doesn't mean the imbalance that caused the disease is magically gone. It just means the organ is no longer there, so it doesn't hurt anymore.

Genuine health involves more than physical processes. Just as we can't treat a single organ as separate from the whole of the body's system, we can't treat our body as separate from the whole of who we are. As embodied beings, we are body, mind, and spirit. When there is an imbalance in one of these aspects, it affects the whole, just as a diseased organ affects the entire body.

Body affects mind and spirit. Spirit affects body and mind. Mind affects body and spirit. Therefore, any illness or difficult symptom or situation in your life requires you to balance the entire system in order to return to optimal function. Vibrational healing seeks to accomplish this by creating balance.

The Process in Action

I'll share a recent personal story of healing so you can get an idea of what this process looks like in action.

Without going into too much detail, I'll tell you that for about six weeks, I dealt with a persistent, severe health issue that affected every single aspect of my life. However, I had a lot on my plate so I told myself I would deal with it later when I had time.

At the time, I was working on two books, I had a conference coming up where I was speaking and teaching four classes, and I had my Nia White Belt training, which was seven long days of classes and intensive movement.

Throughout, the problem persisted and worsened. It

flared significantly and painfully at the most inconvenient times: when I was onstage speaking, when I was socializing, when I was teaching a class, or when I was dancing. During these times, it flared to a point where I couldn't ignore it, and I had to remove myself from what I was doing to rest. My body was desperately trying to get my attention.

Finally after six weeks, I had some downtime, and I asked my body what it was trying to tell me. Lots flooded in, much of it about uncomfortable emotional baggage I'd carried for years. As soon as I pinpointed the issue and gave the intention to release and heal it, my body started to heal, and the issue improved. However, it still lingered. I knew there was one final concrete step I needed to take although I wasn't looking forward to it because it involved me going to someone and admitting I was wrong and had been engaging in emotional bullshit. I approached that person right away the next morning, and the issue was completely gone by that evening. For six weeks I'd struggled with it, and just like that it was gone as if it had never been there in the first place.

During the six weeks of my issue, I would have told you I'd done everything physically possible (short of going to my doctor who would've recommended surgery, of that I've no doubt) to heal my body. However, it wasn't until I dealt with the emotional, vibrational, and spiritual aspects of the issue and followed my intuition about what I needed to do that it cleared up 100 percent. Body, mind, and spirit are intertwined, and each affects the other.

About This Book

I just threw a whole lot of esoteric and spiritual philosophy at you quickly in order to provide background about why and how vibrational healing works. In the chapters that follow, I plan to give you concrete tools and activities in which you can engage in order to raise your vibration, balance energy, and heal.

The first section explains your body's energetic systems with a focus on the chakras and provides a process for identifying issues as they relate to your energetic systems. It also offers a process for healing.

The second section is your vibrational healing toolbox. In it, I discuss the body's various energetic systems and provide you with tools to heal the issues in your life, from physical and mental health struggles to other aspects of your life, such as finances, career, and relationships. You can choose to use as many or as few as you like.

The tools cover an array of practices, attitudes, activities, and healing modalities. Find those that resonate with you and use them as you will. You can use one, a few, or all of the tools as you begin your healing journey.

As you use the tools, I strongly recommend journaling. Allow yourself to truly consider and fully participate in the suggested exercises and activities and write your physical, emotional, mental, and spiritual responses to them. Vibrational healing is part of a process of getting to know yourself so you can balance your body, mind, and spirit.

Section I:
Your Energy Systems

Chapter 1: An Overview of Your Energetic Systems

If you look in the mirror, chances are you see your physical body. You notice skin, hair, and nails. You see a face and some of your sensory organs. You may notice the clothes you wear, your facial expression, your build, and the structure created from what lies under the surface: your muscles, bones, fat, and organs.

We are most acquainted with our physical body because we perceive it through our five senses. We spend a great deal of time tending to our physical needs because they will not be ignored. We need to eat and sleep. We need to move and rest. When we are sick, we need to heal. When we are in pain, we want it to stop. Your physical body's needs are immediate and pressing, and you are always aware of them. Your body contains your various physical systems and organs, such as your nervous system, digestive system, circulatory system, and so on.

Your physical body also includes your brain, which is the embodied component of your mind. You use your brain on a daily basis. It controls multiple bodily functions, both those you control consciously (thinking, speaking, walking, talking, etc.) and those that are automatic (breathing, digestion, heartbeat, etc.). Your brain (and nervous system) is also the part of your body that allows you to perceive physical sensations like pain or pleasure or notice sensory input, such as touch, taste, sight, smell, and sounds. Your brain is part of your mind, but it isn't all of it. Your mind also has a nonphysical element, which is your consciousness. It's the part of you that senses, feels, and dreams. It is the part where ego exists and where the idea of separation and duality takes root. Your mind is what causes you to perceive your existence and experience in three-dimensional space.

Finally, there's a part of you that's completely nonphysical, something you may refer to as your spirit or soul. This is the higher part of you that is eternal. It is multi-dimensional and exists outside of the 3-dimensional space in which your body lives. Spirit is your connection to higher realms including creation, source, God, and Divinity. Spirit is responsible for innate, inspiration, intuition, creativity, love, compassion, kindness, and humility.

All three of these aspects exist in you, and your energetic systems, or energy anatomy, provide the connection between the three: body, mind, and spirit. Your energy systems provide the connection points between the physical and non-physical realms. Your energetic system has three parts, which include your chakras, meridians, and aura.

Aura

Your aura is the energy field that surrounds you. Everything that is alive has an aura including trees, plants, animals, and people. The aura is your energetic imprint, which extends outward from your body. Auras come in different colors that change constantly depending on moods and emotions, illnesses or health, and a zillion other qualities that affect your electromagnetic field. Kirlian photographers can capture images of your aura by subjecting a photographic plate to a strong electric field.

Your aura is both protective and reactive. It reacts to anything that affects your energy, and it also holds energy close to you. Many energy healers start a vibrational healing session by sweeping the aura to cleanse it of any negative energies that have become trapped there.

Your aura has multiple layers and planes that reflect different energetic aspects of your being. Closest to your body is your physical energy aura, which reflects what is happening energetically in your physical body. A little further out is the astral aura, which reflects your emotional state. Next come lower and higher mental auras, each a little further from the body. These reflect the thought patterns of your brain and the thought patterns of your mind. Next is the spiritual aura, which reflects your spiritual aspects, such as your understandings, spiritual learning, and more. In the next layer is information about your dreams and intuition. Finally, the farthest away from the body is the absolute aura plane, a balancing part of your aura that helps integrate all of the other layers. It is in this layer where your entire spiritual blueprint lies. It holds your Akashic DNA. Your *Akash* (or *Akashic record*) is that part of your eternal soul that stores all of your experiences and understandings throughout every incarnation and spiritual evolution from the beginning of your existence through now.

Meridians

Another energetic system that ties your physical to the spiritual is your meridian system. Meridians are a network of nonphysical and physical channels through which your life force energy (sometimes called *chi, qi,* or *prana*) flows. These meridians run through your physical body, and when they become blocked, imbalance can occur. Modalities like acupuncture and acupressure release these blockages and allow the life force energy to flow freely. Activities like yoga and martial arts also work with this life force energy, encouraging it to flow optimally throughout the body to create balance.

Chakras

Chakras are energetic centers that run through your body's core. Energy flows through your chakras, and each has its own energetic imprint. These energetic centers connect the body, mind, and spirit, sharing information and energy between the physical and nonphysical aspects of you. You have seven main chakras, as well as multiple minor chakras. When chakras are blocked, underactive, or overactive, energetic imbalance occurs. Many of the tools and activities we discuss focus on the chakra system.

Chapter 2: A Process for Healing

Caring deeply for yourself requires attention to body, mind, and spirit. You cannot separate the three, as much as you'd like to. Body, mind, and spirit are intertwined, and each affects the other. When you experience a health problem or find dissatisfaction or pain in any aspect of your life in need of healing, you can begin to work with your energetic systems. Noticing there is suffering is the first and most important part of the process.

Tools for Healing

Healing—and what brings it about—is highly individual. However, self-examination is an important tool in your arsenal when you're trying to heal any issue.

Before I get too deeply into the tools, I need to say this: if you are experiencing a life-threatening issue, if you suspect a disease process that requires treatment, or if you are bleeding or broken, working with the emotional and spiritual aspects of your health issue shouldn't override seeking medical care. It's important to your health you seek appropriate medical evaluation and treatment. Then, work with the spiritual and emotional in conjunction with proper health care; it should supplement it, not replace it. Ignoring a medical issue is never a healthy choice. Your body is trying to get your attention. When your body is stabilized, however, you can turn to spiritual and emotional tools to help you find balance.

Step 1: Identify the Issue(s) and Associated Chakra

When faced with an issue in need of healing, whether it is spiritual, mental, emotional, physical, or all of the above, the first place to start is with the chakras because every issue has a chakra association. To do this, you must first identify the areas of concern. If it's physical pain, that's pretty easy to do. You know, for instance, whether your foot or your face hurts, so you can start there. Sometimes, however, the physical symptoms are the last to come as your Divine guidance system prepares to whack you with a two-by-four.

If the issue is mental, emotional, or spiritual, it may take a bit more exploration. When you're feeling out of balance, take a look at the lists of physical, emotional, or mental issues for each chakra and see if one or more of those ring true for you. If one does, start there. Chances are if you identify one of these issues, you will also find a correlation to physical symptoms you've been having, although they may be so mild you barely noticed them.

For example, in the situation I shared about myself in the introduction, what I noticed first was a physical symptom. It was hormonal and was causing major and debilitating symptoms. It's also a problem that had recurred frequently over the past several years, each time more severe than the previous. In fact, once it was so severe it required hospitalization.

Once I identified the physical issue, which was associated with hormones and a certain area of my body, I was also able to identify it was related to my second chakra. From there, I examined the spiritual, emotional, and mental problems that might contribute to or arise from a second chakra imbalance. What I noticed is it wasn't just this physical issue at play and when I looked at it, I realized there wasn't just a single issue occurring related to my second chakra. Not only were my hormones messed up and my body responding, but I discovered some other second chakra emotional concerns I had never examined or dealt with, including thoughts and beliefs about sexuality, prosperity and abundance, and many others. I had a second chakra "cluster," something that's not uncommon. If the energy in a chakra is unbalanced, it often occurs there are multiple aspects of your life related to that chakra in need of attention.

Step Two: Practice Deep Self Honesty Without Judgment: Observe and Notice

As you begin to examine the issues associated with the chakra you've identified, it's time to be very honest with yourself. I know it's difficult to do this without self-judgment, but try to step back, be an observer, and notice the issues without judging them or yourself. Instead, notice how you feel about certain situations, how issues from your past might affect you, how your behaviors and choices may be affecting the issue, etc. This goes beyond physical. It's important you look at mental, emotional, and spiritual issues associated with these chakras, as well.

Keep digging deeply until you've identified the issues affecting that chakra and/or body part. I find there's a click when I hit on the right one - this feeling of *ahhhhh....okay*. It's a knowing, and your body and spirit will send you an undeniable signal you've hit on it. Your Divine guidance system will help you recognize the truth.

Step Three: Ask if You're Ready to Let Go

Ask yourself, *Am I ready to release this, or is it still serving me in some way?* If you feel it still serves you, it's important to examine how and why, and if this choice is truly in your best interests or if it is holding you back from what you feel is your purpose in life. Non-judgment is critical here. As much as you can, do this from the role of the observer. If feelings arise related to the issues you bring up, certainly allow yourself to fully experience those emotions so they don't get stuck in your body and then let them and move through you without self-judgment and with the intention for self-compassion and love. If you are truly still not ready to let this go, then just be with it and notice when it arises in your life and how it affects you. At some point, you may notice it no longer serves you and decide to move on. If and when that occurs, move on to step 4.

Step Four: Set Your Intention to Heal

In self-healing, intention is everything. Noticing is the first step to healing. Letting go is the second. Intending to heal is the next and most powerful. You can do this silently, out loud, while looking in the mirror, in writing, in meditation, or wherever and whenever it feels most appropriate to you. Be as specific as possible. For example, for my second chakra issue, I used the statement, "I notice I am experiencing x, y, and z (my issues) as a result of an imbalanced second chakra, and I choose to heal it."

Step Five: Use Your Tools

Use any of the tools available in this toolbox. Devote 10 to 20 minutes per day to working actively on rebalancing that chakra. It doesn't have to be all in one sitting. You can do it in chunks of time. More severe issues may require a bigger commitment.

Use vibrational healing practices for the affected chakra and all other chakras. Be patient. While healing can occur in an instant, it is more likely it will take some time, so be consistent with your practices. Treat the effected chakra with love and care as you work to strengthen and heal it from the long-term energetic toll the issue has taken.

Use any of the tools available to you to balance all of your chakras. Listen to your intuition and use the forms that feel most appropriate to you. Your Divine guidance system will help you discover what will work best to balance your energy.

Step Six: Continue with Mental, Spiritual, and Emotional Work

As part of your toolbox, you'll find questions for examination that allow you to delve deeply into issues related to your chakras. Work with these questions and be as honest as you can. This will allow you to continue to identify additional sources of the issue. Often, a long-term and persistent issue has multiple sources that reveal themselves to you as if you are peeling away layers. As you discover new layers, you can take the steps necessary for personal healing, whether that is changing your beliefs, making amends to yourself or someone else, sitting down with a professional for talk therapy, or something else. It's important you commit to the process of healing. Without the commitment and work you put into it, healing is unlikely to occur.

Step Seven: Express Gratitude

It's a true effort from your mind, body, and spirit to help you find imbalances and heal them. Give thanks to your body for the warning. Give thanks to your Divine guidance system for assisting. Give thanks to your mind and spirit that you are able to intend to heal. And give thanks to yourself for your willingness to work with the vibrational tools to balance your energetic systems.

Step Eight: Celebrate Your Self Care

This is an intensive process. It's not easy. Certainly taking a pill is easier, but is it really fixing the problem? This process arises from self love and can be the impetus for tremendous spiritual and personal growth. It can remove blockages in your life and allow you to live more fully and vibrantly. It's important to approach it with an attitude of openness and non-judgment, without expectations of results other than those that are in your greatest and highest good.

This deep level of self-care is a beautiful thing, and you deserve to love and care for yourself in such a way. Celebrate the self-love this takes, and offer gratitude to every aspect of yourself—body, mind, and spirit—that you are embarking on the process of deep self-healing.

Chicken or Egg?

Imbalances in the chakras can cause physical, mental, spiritual, and emotional issues. Likewise, physical, mental, emotional, and spiritual issues can cause imbalances in your chakras. Each affects the other, but regardless of which causes which, the solutions are the same: to acknowledge and heal the underlying imbalance and remove its causes using the above process.

Chapter 3 – The Chakras

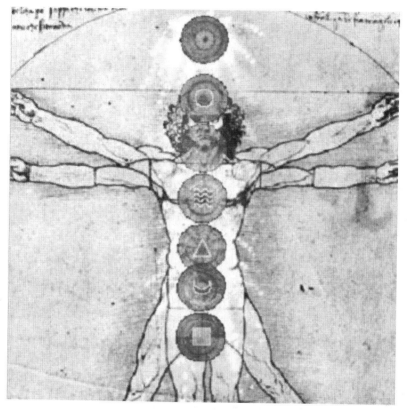

Your body has seven major energy centers called chakras that run through its core. It also has multiple minor chakras (such as in the palms of your hands). However, for our purposes we'll focus on the seven major energetic centers. Each chakra is a rotating wheel of light and energy associated with a different color. Each chakra has its own energy. Above is an illustration of your seven major chakras. Each vibrates at a different frequency and affects different aspects of your physical, emotional, mental, and spiritual health. Chakras may become blocked so energy is unable to flow through them, or they may become overactive or underactive and create imbalances. Imbalances in your chakras can cause an array of physical, mental, emotional, and spiritual complaints.

Root Chakra – Muladhara

Your root chakra, also called muldahara, sits at the base of your spine. When you sit, you sit on your root chakra. It is associated with the color red.

Just as the root chakra is the foundation of your chakra system (it sits at the base), it's also representative of the foundation of your spiritual, emotional, and mental health. It is the chakra through which you ground yourself – that is, you connect yourself to the Earth and to all that is terrestrial. The root chakra is your source of connection to life on Earth, and it connects your earthy choices and decisions to your higher self.

Physical Health

Your root chakra (also called your first chakra, or some people call it the base chakra) affects the following physical aspects of the body:

- Legs and feet
- Hips and knees
- Bowels and rectum
- Bones
- Sacrum and coccyx (base of the spine)
- Immune system
- Sciatic nerve

- Prostate

When you notice illnesses with any of these areas, they are likely connected to an energetic imbalance in the root chakra. So some (but certainly not all) health issues related to the root chakra include:

- Sciatica
- Swelling in the legs
- Foot pain, fallen arches, plantar fasciitis, Achilles tendon issues
- Knee problems
- Osteoporosis
- Autoimmune disorders or immune system dysfunction
- Enlarged prostate
- Constipation
- Irritable bowel syndrome (IBS)
- Crohn's disease
- Restless leg syndrome

Mental Health

Root chakra imbalances can generate the following mental health issues. Likewise, these concerns can also cause overactive or underactive energy in the root chakra:

- Depression
- Multiple personalities
- Addictions
- Compulsions and obsessions (or OCD)
- Anxiety
- Nightmares
- Eating disorders

Emotional Health

The following emotional issues can cause root chakra energetic disturbances or vice versa (that is, root chakra energetic disturbances can cause the following emotional issues):

- Feelings of lack of security – physically, emotionally, financially, etc. (often arising from childhood)
- Issues regarding personal safety
- Safety of your family
- Standing up for yourself
- Supporting yourself and others (financially, emotionally, etc.)
- Loyalty
- Your place in the family or tribe
- Meeting, earning, or receiving the minimum requirements/necessities to live
- Familial teachings and beliefs
- Betrayal
- Abandonment
- Superstitions
- Traditions and rituals from your tribal background (this can be social groups, family, church groups, etc. – any and all tribes to which you did or do belong)
- Code of honor/sense of justice and morals
- Hurt from family relationships
- Stability
- Fear
- Trust
- Instincts
- Family wounds (from childhood)
- Abundance and lack
- Need for domination or control
- Materialism

Spiritual Health

Your root chakra is the energy center of grounding. If you are ungrounded, chances are there is an energetic imbalance in your root chakra.

Sacral Chakra – Svadisthana

Your second chakra, also called the sacral or spleen chakra, sits in your core beneath your belly button. It is associated with the color orange.

Just as the chakra is centered in your belly, so is your personal power centered in this chakra. It is your source of creativity and sexuality, and it relates to issues of personal power, finance, and interpersonal relationships.

Physical Health
Your sacral chakra affects the following areas of your body:

- Large intestine
- Sexual organs
- Pelvis
- Appendix
- Bladder
- Lower spine and back

Health issues associated with your second chakra include:

- Bladder infections
- Issues with urination
- Appendicitis
- Lower back pain
- Menstrual problems
- Sexual dysfunction
- PMS
- Difficult menopause
- Fibroids

Mental and Emotional Health
Mental health issues related to second chakra imbalances

41

include:

- Codependency
- Lack of independence
- Sexual addiction or frigidity
- Guilt and blame
- Victimization
- Prosperity and money issues
- Lack of boundaries
- Lack of or excessive ethics
- Sociopathy or psychopathy
- Histrionic personality disorder (HPD)
- Manipulation or easily manipulated
- Excessive risk taking or unwillingness to take risks
- Creativity or lack thereof
- Indecision
- Failed relationships or over attachment in relationships
- Detachment
- Jealousy or envy
- Greed
- PCOS

Spiritual Health

Your second chakra is the source of your emotions and your connection to others in one-on-ne relationships. It allows you to see (or blocks you from seeing) the inherent spiritual value in every relationship you have with another.

Solar Plexus Chakra - Manipura

Your third chakra, also called the solar plexus or naval chakra, is associated with a sense of self and building self-worth and self-esteem. It is in the third chakra where you form your identity separate from your family, tribe, or society. It is located at the base of your sternum and is associated with the color yellow or gold. This is where you create your sense of me-ness, and it is where your (necessary for the human experience) belief in your separation from everyone and everything else exists.

Physical Health
Physical areas and organs associated with your solar plexus chakra include:

- Stomach and abdomen
- Kidneys
- Adrenals
- Spleen
- Gallbladder
- Liver
- Lower middle back
- Duodenum

Health issues that may arise with solar plexus chakra imbalance include:

- Kidney stones and infection
- Adrenal insufficiency, exhaustion, or malfunction
- Gallstones
- Hepatitis and liver disease
- Diabetes and hypoglycemia
- Mid back pain
- Ulcers
- Pancreatitis
- Indigestion/GERD
- Hiatal hernia
- Digestive issues, such as gastroparesis
- Addison's disease

Mental/Emotional Health
Mental and emotional health issues that may arise include:

- Anorexia or bulimia
- Lack of self-confidence or self-esteem
- Body dysmorphia or anxiety/upset about physical appearance
- Narcissistic personality disorder/narcissism
- Borderline personality disorder
- Pathological or compulsive lying
- Fear of rejection
- Powerlessness
- Inability to accept criticism
- Lack of courage or ambition
- Overambitious
- Overly critical
- Approval seeking
- Lack of self-respect/self love
- Lack of responsibility (or hyper responsibility)
- Fantasizing about life being completely different
- Envy and resentment of others
- Attention seeking behaviors

Spiritual Health

Spiritually, your third chakra is about accepting responsibility for the creation of your life through your thoughts, words, actions, and choices.

Heart Chakra – Anahata

Your heart chakra, also known as the thymus or fourth chakra, serves as the connection between your body chakras (one through three) and your mind/spirit chakras (five through seven). It is where love exists in your body; unconditional love, romantic love, familial love, and universal love. The heart chakra is located in the center of your chest and associated with the color green.

Physical Health

Your heart chakra affects the following body parts, organs, and systems:

- Heart
- Lungs
- Circulation
- Ribs
- Middle back
- Arms, shoulders, and hands
- Thymus
- Breasts/chest
- Diaphragm

Physical issues associated with your heart chakra include:

- Blood and circulation problems
- Heart disease
- Blood vessel disease
- Lung disease
- Pneumonia
- Breast problems, such as cysts, lumps, and cancers
- Mid and upper back problems
- Congestive heart failure
- Bronchitis
- Chronic cough
- High blood pressure
- Asthma

Emotional/Mental Health

Emotional and mental issues associated with a heart chakra imbalance include:

- Bitterness
- Grief
- Forgiveness or lack thereof
- Self-centeredness

- Loneliness
- Inability to commit
- Difficulty with relationships
- Being abusive
- Lack of compassion or empathy
- Feeling unworthy of love
- Inability to love
- Competitive
- Deceitful
- Manipulative
- Inability to bond with others

Spiritual Health

Spiritually, your heart is the source of unconditional, universal, spiritual love which serves as the balance point between higher realms and physical realms.

Throat Chakra - Vishuddha

Your throat or fifth chakra sits at the base of your throat just above your thyroid. It is associated with the color blue.

Your throat chakra is all about communication and speaking your truth, as well as surrendering your personal (ego-driven) will to the plan your Divine self has for you.

Physical Health

Your throat chakra affects the following body parts, organs, and systems:

- Throat
- Thyroid
- Parathyroid
- Hypothalamus
- Esophagus

- Neck
- Jaw
- Tongue
- Teeth
- Gums

Physical health issues that might be associated with this chakra include:

- TMJ and jaw pain
- Gum disease
- Hypo or hyperthyroidism
- Hashimoto's disease
- Grave's disease
- Difficulty swallowing
- Laryngitis
- Swollen glands in the neck
- Hypothalamic dysfunction
- Canker sores
- Dental issues
- Halitosis
- Upper respiratory infection
- Tonsillitis

Emotional and Mental Health

Mental and emotional health issues can arise from imbalances of the throat chakra, such as:

- Inability or unwillingness to express yourself
- Not bringing creative ideas to fruition or not acting on creativity
- Miscommunication or inability to communicate
- Aphasia
- Talking without listening
- Excessive talkativeness
- Being wishy washy or indecisive

Spiritual Health

Your throat chakra is where your creative ideas come into expression, and it also governs your ability to listen and speak clearly in ways that create what you truly desire in the universe.

Third Eye Chakra – Ajna

Your third eye chakra—also known as the sixth or pineal chakra—is your center of intuition. It is associated with the color violet or indigo and is located in the center of the forehead just above the bridge of your nose. As the source of your intuition and intellectual ability, this is the energy center through which your higher self can communicate with you. It is also the center of psychic energy, as well as reasoning and intellect.

Physical Health

Organs and body parts and systems associated with the third eye chakra include:

- Brain
- Pineal gland
- Eyes
- Ears
- Nose
- Pituitary gland
- Face

Health issues potentially associated with the third eye chakra include:

- Stroke and brain hemorrhage
- Alzheimer's
- Memory problems

- Dementia
- Seizures and epilepsy
- Neurological disorders
- Bells palsy
- Ocular issues
- Hearing issues
- Learning disabilities
- Issues of the entire spine
- Cognitive issues
- Sinus problems
- Chronic congestion
- Headaches (including migraines)
- Visual disturbances
- Insomnia
- Brain fog

Mental and Emotional Health

Mental or emotional issues associated with third eye imbalances include:

- Being closed minded
- Overthinking
- Lack of emotional intelligence
- Inability to learn from experience
- Negative patterns in life
- Fixed beliefs or lack of beliefs
- Delusions
- Mental health disorders such as schizophrenia, bipolar disorder, or schizoaffective disorder
- Stress
- Grandiosity
- Lack of common sense
- Lack of intuition
- Lack of equilibrium

Spiritual Health

Spiritually, your third eye chakra opens you to universal

wisdom as communicated by your higher self and your Divine guidance system. It connects you to Divinely inspired intuition.

Crown Chakra – Sahasrara

Your crown chakra, also known as the seventh chakra, is just above the top of your head. It is associated with the colors pink, white, or violet, and it is your connection to higher spiritual realms. It is through this chakra you connect with Divinity, your higher self, and Source. This chakra allows spirituality to become an important part of your life, and through its energy, you proceed to enlightenment and ascension, which is the ultimate state for every embodied being.

Physical Health

Physically, your crown chakra is associated with three systems: your skeletal system, your skin, and your muscular system. Therefore, health issues that arise with these systems as a whole, such as bone cancer, skin cancer, or ALS, are associated with the crown chakra. Health problems with nonspecific causes may also be associated with the crown chakra, such as chronic fatigue or exhaustion, sensory integration disorder, or environmental hypersensitivity.

Mental, Emotional and Spiritual Health

This chakra relates to mental, emotional, and spiritual health issues like trust, philanthropy and social justice, spirituality, and faith. Spiritually, it is your source of connection that allows you to develop a personal relationship with a higher power, see the Divine in others, and be present in the moment.

Section II
Your Vibrational Healing Toolbox

Chapter 4 – Vibration and Healing

The chapters that follow offer an array of tools to help you change the vibration of your chakras and other energetic systems to assist in creating balance so you can heal. All are designed to affect your vibration and free blockages, temper an overabundance of energy, and increase energy flow where it is moving slowly.

Feeling the Vibes

Have you ever said, "I like her. She's got a good vibe?" Have you ever walked into a room and decided you either love or hate the vibe? Everything and everyone has its own unique vibration. In fact, even though most people don't believe they are able to, almost anyone can feel something's vibration.

Try this. Rub your hands together vigorously for a full 60 seconds. Now, pull them slowly apart. Do you feel that energy zapping between your hands? That's vibration. Pull your hands apart slowly until the sensation stops. Now, close your eyes and slowly bring them back together again until you can feel the tingling once more.

This is a simple exercise I use in my classes that allows people to actually feel vibration, and anyone can do it. In the exercise we're using a physical act (rubbing the hands together) to generate friction and energy that continues for a time after we stop and pull our hands apart.

All vibration works in a similar manner. All matter has a vibration, because all matter is made up of vibrating strings of energy. All living creatures also have vibration, not only from their cells and electrical systems, but also through their spiritual and energetic systems. Nobody's vibration feels quite the same as anyone else's.

Everyone has a certain *feel* to them when you think of them. For instance, have you ever been sitting at home and noticed a sensation only to have your mom pop into your mind, and a minute later the phone rings and it's your mom. Just before you thought of and identified your mom by name, there was a split-second sensation you experienced that caused you to think of her. That's your mom's vibe.

Now think about somebody you loved a long time ago whom you haven't seen for years – perhaps a first love or a childhood best friend. Close your eyes and allow yourself to truly sense that person. Do you feel a familiarity there that goes beyond your physical visualization of that person? That familiar sensation is their vibe. It's how you can sense someone looking at you across a room when your back is turned. It's how you can meet a total stranger and feel an instant connection, only to have them become a lifelong friend. It's how you can meet another total stranger and without even thinking feel, *Nope, not you* because something about they way the feel just doesn't…well, it doesn't vibe.

Sensing vibrations is one way your higher self communicates with you and helps guide you along the path of your highest and greatest good. Can you think of a time when you've met someone, ignored an "off" vibe because you didn't want to be a judgmental jerk, befriended that person anyway, and then lived to regret it? (Boy have I done that a few times.) Have you ever had an icky feeling about a situation (maybe a new job or some activity) but ignored it and gone ahead and took the job or engaged in the activity only to totally and completely regret it? (Oh yeah – I've done this, too). This is your higher self communicating with you through subtle vibrations to help guide you. It's up to you whether you listen, but it's a pretty accurate guidance system.

Everyone and Everything Vibrates

While it isn't necessary to actually feel vibration to participate in vibrational healing, it is important to understand this one concept: everyone and everything has a vibration. Your thoughts have vibration. So do your words, actions, emotions, and intentions. Creativity—either expressed or squandered—has a vibration. The food you eat, the clothes you wear, and the things with which you surround yourself do, as well.

Therefore, everything you do, every thought you have, every choice you make, every word you speak, every action you take, every item you touch, every person you encounter, every emotion you feel, and every attitude you choose has the capacity to affect your vibration as well as everything around it.

Energetically, different parts of you have different vibrational frequencies. For example, each of your chakras vibrates at its own frequency that affects the overall vibration of the entire system, which is your body, mind, and spirit. Likewise, every individual on the planet has its own unique vibration which in turn, affects the vibration of the entire planet. And across the universe, every planet, star, solar system, meteor, and other celestial body all has its own unique vibration which affects the vibration of the entire universe. Since as we rise in vibration, we come closer to enlightenment, doing things to raise your own personal vibration has a major effect on the totality of everything in the entire universe. You are far more important to the universe than you could ever imagine, and your thoughts, words, and actions have the capacity to raise or lower the vibration of the entire universe. Never think you aren't important. You are, and you're so much more gloriously Divine than you know.

Receiving Vibration

You can absorb vibration through your five senses (sight, smell, touch, taste, sound). You can also absorb it into your body, even if you can't sense it. Likewise, you can receive and affect vibration through activities such as prayer, meditation, and movement. You can also receive or affect it with the thoughts you think, the words you speak, the judgments you make, the emotions you have, the actions you take, the love or fear you hold, the way you treat others, the way you treat yourself, and the way you allow others to treat you.

How the Tools Affect Vibration

The tools that follow all affect vibration. Some, like crystals and sound healing, do it through the principle of entrainment. They vibrate at a certain frequency, and that frequency causes nearby systems to synchronize. You can find an excellent illustration of entrainment with metronomes. When mechanical metronomes are set near one another all ticking at different tempos, eventually they all entrain and synchronize to the same tempo. Entrainment helps balance your energetic systems and chakras by resonating with the frequency you need those chakras to hold in order to create balance.

Other tools, such as meditation, prayer, affirmations, and visualization, affect vibration by helping you to raise your overall frequency and release blockages in your energetic systems.

Food and movement allow you to physically move energy and add energy to your body. Herbs and essential oils help you mentally and emotionally raise your vibration and also create entrainment when dealing with specific energies.

How to Use the Tools

There is no right or wrong way to use the tools that follow. I'll offer suggestions, which you can either take or discard as you wish. Listen to your intuition and do what feels right. This is your Divine guidance system gently nudging you in a direction that serves your highest and greatest good.

Familiarize yourself with the tools. Then, decide what's right for you. If one tool doesn't seem to work or isn't available to you, try another. Your goal is to forge the path that is best for you using any tools available.

Chapter 5 – Awareness and Intention

All process of balancing or raising vibration starts with awareness and intention. Many chakra (and other energetic) imbalances arise from lack of awareness about ourselves.

Being Aware

Awareness is a simple concept that can be challenging in practice. Masters and sages suggest it's ideal for embodied humans to live in a state of awareness focused in the present moment and noticing only what happens right now without projecting into the future or fretting about the past.

In his book *Power of Now,* author Eckhart Tolle says all human pain comes from projecting into the future or thinking about the past, and if we just live in this moment of now, we will not only be free from pain but also exist in a state of bliss. Tolle further contends the past and the future are only illusions, and now is the only true reality.

Many spiritual works discuss this concept, as well. In the Kryon channelings by Lee Carrol, Kryon frequently shares that our higher selves only live in the moment of now and there is no concrete past or future because those concepts exist only as probabilities. As we move through our lives—either as embodied spirits or as pieces of the Divine on the soul plane— our experience arises from where in that sea of probabilities we place our attention.

It's a little like a game on a DVD or computer. Within that software, the entire game exists as code that offers an array of probabilities. All of the probabilities for that game exist in the software, but a player will not experience every single probability as they move through the game. Instead, he or she will only experience what comes in the path they play based on the choices they make as they play it. While the entire game exists as a whole with multiple options and probabilities that could occur, the player has a singular experience that is occurring in the moment as he or she makes choices.

On a much grander and more intricate scale, our embodied lives are like that computer game. Every probability and outcome exists, but the path we experience and the probabilities we bring into being in our physical experience come from the choices we make and where we place our attention in each moment. The more aware we are, the more likely we are to make choices and take actions that bring our attention to the probabilities we experience as being more favorable.

Living Awareness

Living in awareness takes work, and for many people it's only achievable in small moments of present time focus. However, you can make as much of your life as possible a living awareness where you are focused only in the moment of now.

Living awareness can take many forms, but mostly it's about attention and focusing on sensation in the moment. It involves quieting your mind as much as possible and when thoughts or emotions do arise, allowing them to do so without judgment. And, as you live, pay attention to things like movement, feelings, or physical sensations. Do so without judgment and with pleasure.

For example, suppose you are washing the dishes. Now I don't know about you, but when I wash dishes I've got a whole story going on. Some of it is about how much I hate to do dishes and how I'm the only one in the house who ever seems to actually do them. When I am in living awareness, however, I let that story drift away. Instead, I notice the sights, sounds, smells, and textures, as well as how my body feels and moves, and the sensations related to ambient energies such as heat, air conditioning, or sunlight. If thoughts arise, I allow them without attachment or judgment. Inside I am as still as I can be while I focus on what I am doing. I may notice the warmth of the water on my hands, the scent of the soap, or the sunlight coming through my kitchen window making patterns on the wall behind the sink.

When you are in awareness, your mind is quiet and you exist in the role of both the person who is living in your body in each moment as well as one who is observing from a higher plane. In this state, you notice without judgment all the things that arise.

It's natural for thoughts and emotions to rise in our minds, even when we are practicing living awareness. It's also natural for us to attach to those thoughts, follow them, and get all riled up as we tell ourselves stories. One trick I use for dealing with these thoughts and noticing them instead of attaching to them is the chalkboard trick.

As I work and pay attention to what I am doing, I notice the thoughts that arise in my mind. Once the thought has fully formed, I momentarily visualize it on a chalkboard and then picture an eraser wiping it away. I do this for each thought as it arises. I allow it, notice it, and then erase it and return my attention to what I am doing. I try not to get caught up in any single thought. I can use this while I'm doing the dishes, dancing, talking a walk on a sunny afternoon, or sitting outside in the sunlight listening to the birds singing. In this way, I don't allow my thoughts to distract me from enjoying the moment of now and existing in my state of living awareness.

Cultivating Energetic Awareness

You can also exist in a state of energetic awareness. This is a tool I use to help as I discover energetic imbalances and work to heal them. Cultivating energetic awareness is a process in which you examine where there are imbalances and determine how your spiritual, mental, and emotional issues may contribute to or create those imbalances. Creating this awareness is the first step in finding balance.

Using a process of inquiry is one of your best tools for discovering the source of these imbalances. Below, you will find questions you can ask yourself and answer honestly as you work with energetic imbalances. They are organized by chakra, so if you are aware of an imbalance in one of your chakras, you can start with those questions. I recommend keeping a journal of your responses.

Root Chakra
- What beliefs do you hold about yourself that came from your family?
- What beliefs do you hold about others that came from your family?
- How did your upbringing affect the way you view yourself?
- Today, do you feel you are living your life in harmony with what your family taught you, or do you feel as if you have chosen a different path? How do you feel about that? How do you feel about your place in your family of birth now as a result of your choice of beliefs?
- What superstitions do you have? Where did they come from? How important are they to you?

- How stable do you feel your life is? What would it take to make you feel more stable?
- How do you feel about the foundation you have created for your life? Do you feel like you are on a solid foundation? Is it perhaps too solid (are you unmoving, inflexible, and unwilling to change)? Is it not solid enough? Why? What would it take to make it comfortable for you?
- What pain are you still carrying from your childhood? How does it affect you in your day to day life? How does it affect your interactions with others and your worldview? How would you be different if you released the pain?
- Is your spiritual/religious belief system consistent with your upbringing? How do you feel about that? Do you feel alienated from your tribe of origin if your belief system is different from theirs?
- What scares you the most? Do you have any deep, dark, hidden fears you don't want to admit to? How much power or influence do those fears have over your thoughts, words, and actions?
- How trusting are you in relationships? How much do you trust in the benevolence of life in the universe? How did your upbringing affect this trust or lack thereof?
- How important are material things to you? Can you easily let go of material things, or are they as important or more important than non-material things in your life? If they are important, why? What would happen if you no longer had them?
- What teachings and traditions do you feel it is important to pass on to your children? Why?
- Do you have a solid code of honor? How firmly do you hold it? What might make you compromise it? How do you feel when you compromise your code of honor?

Sacral Chakra

- Are you creative? What makes you creative? How do you define it? Do you follow through on your creative ideas?
- Do you listen to your gut or ignore it? What happens when you listen? What happens when you ignore it? Do you trust your gut feelings?
- How truthful are you? Do you ever exaggerate or lie in order to make yourself appear better or more interesting to someone else? Do you even recognize if you do this, or is it automatic? What would happen if you were 100 percent authentic and didn't embellish the truth?
- Do you keep promises to yourself and others? What promises are you unlikely to keep that you make to yourself? What promises are you unlikely to keep that you make to other people? Why do you break your promises, and how do you feel when you do? What would happen if you kept your word?
- If you do break promises to yourself or others, what prompts it? What do you feel justifies you breaking your promises? Is it an act of self preservation?
- What is your relationship to your sexuality? Do you have sexual hang-ups? What are they and how do they affect you? Are you able to express yourself freely through your sexuality?
- Do you use your sexuality to gain power and control? How and why does this manifest? How do you feel when you do it? What would happen if you stopped using your sexuality as a way of controlling another person or situation?
- What are your feelings about wealth and prosperity? Do you feel money and possessions are somehow not spiritual? What drives this belief?
- Do you use your material wealth as a means of control or manipulation? How? Why do you do this?

- Do you engage in "lack" consciousness? In other words, how often do you catch yourself believing there is not enough to go around, and for you to have something means someone else cannot have it? What drives this belief? Do you think it's true? What are some reasons why it might not be true?
- What are your ethics regarding money and power? Do you engage in behaviors to claim money and power where you have to justify actions you would see as less than ethical in others?
- Do you make choices and decisions that arise from fear about your survival? Do these choices fit within your ethical framework? Would you be upset if someone else made the same decision, yet you feel as if you have to justify your own anyway? How does it feel when you make choices that don't fit your ethics out of fear for survival?
- Do your fears control you, or do you control your fears? How?
- Are you pursuing your goals and dreams? If no, why not? Is there something you feel is blocking you from doing so?
- Are you decisive? When you have difficulty making a decision, why? What causes the difficulty? On the other hand, do you decide too quickly? What keeps you from careful consideration?
- Are you jealous of what others have? How do you feel when you experience jealousy? What makes you jealous? Why do you feel you can't have the same thing someone else has that you might be jealous of?
- Do you have firm boundaries? Are you able to tell people no? How do you feel when you don't set firm boundaries?

Solar Plexus Chakra
- What value and worth do you believe you bring to the world? Do you believe your value is inherent, or do you

think you have to do something to be valuable? Where does this belief come from?

- Do you like yourself? Do you frequently say or think negative things about yourself? Why? How do you feel when you do? How would you feel if you stopped?
- In what ways do you define yourself? What are your judgments about these definitions? Are there ways you can define yourself without the value judgments? Which feels better – those definitions attached to judgments or those without?
- What makes you feel powerless? How do you react when you feel that way?
- What don't you like about yourself? Why don't you like it? What would it take for you to like it?
- How critical are you of other people and situations? Are you judgmental? What stories do you tell yourself about other people? Why are you critical? Do you see any of the behaviors you criticize in others in yourself? How does that make you feel?
- When you make a mistake, do you attempt to cover it up or do you admit it and apologize? If you have trouble admitting you were wrong, why is this? What would it take to make you be able to do this? What is the worst thing that would happen if you admitted you were wrong?
- How well do you take care of your physical, spiritual, mental, and emotional needs? If you think you could do better, why aren't you taking care of yourself to the standard you believe you should? What steps could you take to help you care for yourself more effectively?
- Are you able to meet your own needs? In what areas are you deficient?
- How much do you seek the approval of others? What behaviors do you engage in when you seek approval? How do you feel when you don't receive someone else's approval?

- When you are interacting with others, are you busy thinking about whether they approve of you and doing things to get them to like you, or are you authentically engaging? How authentic are you in your interactions with others? If you are inauthentic, why do you think this is?
- Do you put the care of others over caring for yourself? If so, why? What would it take for you to be more focused on caring for yourself?
- Are you able to receive? When someone offers you something, is your first response to say no? Why do you think this is? What would happen if you opened yourself up to receiving?
- Do you feel you respect yourself? Why or why not? What would you need to do to gain your own respect?

Heart Chakra
- Is there anyone in your life you believe you love unconditionally? What does unconditional love look like to you?
- Do you believe someone loves you unconditionally? How do you feel when another puts conditions on love? How do you feel when you put conditions on love?
- Are you holding on to bitterness or grief from the past? How does it affect you? What would it take for you to let it go?
- How are your interpersonal relationships? Are they fulfilling and satisfying or do they leave you wanting more? What do you consider the perfect loving relationship would look like? If you don't have it, what would it take to get it?
- If you have pain from the past, are you able to let it go or do you use it to control others? How do you use your wounds to benefit yourself?
- Do you allow other people to use their emotional pain to manipulate you? How do you feel when that

happens? What would happen if you didn't allow the manipulation?

- Are you able to forgive? What does forgiveness mean to you? If you are unable to forgive, why? What would happen if you did?
- Who do you need to forgive you? Why do you need the forgiveness? Can you forgive yourself? Would you forgive another for the same reasons you feel you need forgiveness?
- What does compassion mean to you? Do you think you are a compassionate person? Why or why not? What would it take for you to be more compassionate? Would others describe you as compassionate?
- Are you abusive (physically, verbally, emotionally, etc.)? Why? What causes you to become abusive? How do you feel when you behave in a way that is abusive? What would it take you to stop?

Throat Chakra

- Do you freely express yourself? If you don't, what is stopping you?
- How well do you listen to and hear others? Are conversations with you two-way, or are you so busy formulating your response you don't hear what the other person is saying? Why do you think this is? What would happen if you listened fully before formulating a response?
- Do you think you are strong-willed or weak willed? What does strong-willed look like? Do you see it as a positive or a negative? How do you assert your will, and how do you feel when others assert their will?
- Do you feel you have willpower? Why or why not? What affects your willpower? How do you feel when you don't have it?
- Do you act on the inner guidance you receive? Do you listen when your inner self is trying to tell you

something or do you ignore it? What happens when you listen, and what happens when you ignore it?

- Do you bring your creative ideas into action and express them? Why or why not?
- Are you able to surrender ego needs to Divine will? Why or why not?
- Are you decisive or wishy washy? Why? Under which circumstances are you decisive? Under which circumstances are you wishy washy?
- Do you speak your truth or hold it back? What would it take for you to speak your truth?
- Do you give voice to your thoughts, beliefs, and emotions? How do you feel when you allow yourself a voice? How do you feel when you don't?
- Do you speak out about issues that are important to you, such as issues of social justice? If you don't, what is keeping you from doing so? How would it feel to express yourself in this way?
- Do you engage in some creative form of self-expression? If yes, what is it? If so, why not? What would it take to allow yourself some form of self-expression? How would you feel if you could fully express yourself?

Third Eye Chakra

- Are you intuitive? Do you listen to the voice of intuition or ignore it? What happens when you do either?
- How do you feel about your own intuition? Do you believe in it or think it is bunk? Why?
- Are you overly analytical? Do you feel you think too much? How do you use the workings of your brain to block yourself in your life?
- Are you able to quiet your mind? Do you feel you have any control over your thoughts, or do you believe your thoughts think you? Why? What would it take to change this?

- Do you use intellectual thoughts as a way to separate yourself from your spiritual or emotional sides? When do you do this? Why do you think you do this? What is driving your need to create a sense of separation from these things?
- How judgmental are you?
- Are you open or close-minded? How do you react when faced with evidence that runs counter to your beliefs?
- How willing are you to listen to the ideas and beliefs of others without judgment? Do the ideas and beliefs of others threaten you? Why?
- How emotionally mature are you? Do you control your emotional reactions or do they control you? Do you allow your emotions to surface and allow yourself to feel them, or do you close yourself off to them?
- Do you notice any negative patterns in your life? What are they? What do you think causes them? What do you think it would take to change them?
- How realistic is your view of yourself? Do you see yourself as more special than others or do you see others as more special than you? How do these beliefs manifest in your life?
- Do you have common sense? If you lack it, how does this lack affect your life?
- When you want to change, do you act on it? If not, what keeps you from making the changes you know you need to?

Crown Chakra
- Do you seek guidance from a higher power? Do you follow it?
- How deeply rooted is your spiritual belief system? Do you believe your spiritual beliefs are more "right" than someone else's who has different beliefs?
- Are you open to different spiritual paths, or do you stick with one out of tradition? How open are you to new

spiritual ideas? What would happen if you allowed yourself to consider them?

- What questions about your life do you have for the Divine? Are there answers the Divine could offer that would satisfy you?
- If you could talk to your God, what would you have Him/Her tell you? How would your life change if you could have two-way conversations with a higher power?
- Do you believe you have conversations with a higher power? If so, how do you feel about them?
- Do you engage in any type of a spiritual practice like meditation or prayer? Why or why not? If you have started and then stopped such a practice, why did you stop?
- Do you believe God hears your prayers?
- Do you believe God/Source/Divine is capricious or behaves in predictable ways? Do you assign human traits to a higher power?
- Do you believe the universe is benevolent or unkind? How do these beliefs affect your choices and behaviors?
- Are you aware of your own Divinity? If so, how does that manifest in your life?
- Do you have fears related to a deeper relationship with the Divine or discovering your own Divinity? What are those fears?

Working with Intention

I often tell my classes intention is everything. Intent is an important tool in your vibrational toolbox because when you set your intent on something and state that intent, your thoughts, words and actions—which are the three things you need for creation—flow from it.

In fact, if you use only one vibrational healing tool, intention is it. Stating your intention is incredibly powerful, so stating the intention to balance and heal can set the wheels of healing in motion.

In order for intent to begin to manifest changes in your life, however, it must be something you truly plan to do, and you've got to mean it. You need to feel your intent deeply in order for it to be effective. And then, you can use it as a powerful tool to aid in vibrational healing.

While powerful, this tool is incredibly simple. Decide what you intend, state your intent, and then act from it. You can state your intent once or reset it daily. You can think about it multiple times a day, focus on it in meditation, chant it as a mantra, or turn it into affirmations. You can write it in your journal or reflect on it each night before you go to sleep. You can whisper it as a prayer or tell everyone you meet what your intent is. The trick is to truly mean it, and then align your thoughts, words, and actions with that intent so you can make it manifest in your life. And if your desire and intent changes, don't be so stuck in an old intent that you let a new one fall by the wayside. Never attach, because attachment leads to stagnation.

Chapter 6: Recognizing and Healing Projections and Judgments

As embodied humans, we have a propensity to be less than honest with ourselves. It's not that we're dirty, no good, rotten liars. However, our survival instinct, the filters we have in place, and our honest desire to be good people often causes us to not recognize our own character flaws while noticing just how blaring everyone else's are.

Discovering Judgment

Judgement of yourself or others (whether positive or negative) is one of the biggest blocks to creating energetic balance in your life. However, as humans we tend to be incredibly judgmental. We do this for a multitude of reasons, but the single biggest one is this: ego. So firmly are we rooted in the illusion of separation and duality that we judge others in order to define them as different from ourselves.

When we judge others, we are creating more separation and pulling ourselves further from the Source. When we judge ourselves, we are replaying scripts from the learning and conditioning we've received throughout our lives from other people, family, tribes, society as a whole, our religious upbringing, our educational process, the media, and many other sources.

Often in order to quiet the voice of judgment we have about ourselves, we instead project those judgments onto other people. Although in a Divine sense we have no separation from everyone else, as embodied humans with egos all we see is separation. And it's far easier to judge someone else than to see in ourselves the aspects we judge so harshly in others.

Understanding Projection

Projection is human nature. It's a protective mechanism, and it's how we hide from what we perceive to be our own flaws.

The trick to starting to remove projections and judgments is to acknowledge you do it, to recognize when you do, and to try to stop those thought processes as they occur. In other words, listen to your thoughts—even those that flash through your head for a split second—and notice your judgments about yourself and others. Then, when you catch yourself judging, see if you can change the thought to one that is without judgment. In other words, be aware of your judgments and have the intention to release them.

Recognizing your judgments and projections can help you identify issues that are causing you imbalance and distress. When you notice you are judging another person or projecting something onto them, take the time to discover what it is you are judging and what is unhealed in yourself that is causing you to judge them and project. Once you've identified those issues, take them to the chakras and notice which chakra the beliefs are likely to be associated with.

A Real Life Example of Projection and Judgment

I'll give you an example from my own life. Judgment is something I've worked on intensely for years. I'm better at being aware of my judgments, but sometimes they still catch me by surprise.

I work as an editor for a few different publications and websites. In the past few months, I've been struggling with one of my writers. I don't really know much about this writer other than through the communications I've had with her and the work she's submitted to me. Much of that work has been sub-par containing grammar, spelling, and factual errors, poor quality of writing, and a clear lack of understanding (or perhaps concern) about who the reading audience is and what types of information they might find the most beneficial.

Initially in my communications with her, my intent was to help her polish her writing so she could improve as a writer, and the quality of the content would meet the submission requirements set forth by the publication for which I was editing. I tried to keep my feedback upbeat and positive with a sense of, *We're all in this together! Let's make article of the highest value to our readers we can.*

The writer would then re-submit with almost no changes, ignoring the feedback I'd offered (although writing to editor feedback was one of the requirements for acceptance of the articles), and making one or two quick and easy changes while still leaving the grammar and spelling errors, content omissions, inaccuracies, etc. For each article, I would go back and forth several times with the writer. Each time, my feedback grew a little less collaborative and friendly and a little terser.

After a few rounds (of which I made my managing editor aware so she would know what was going on with the writer – one of the requirements of my job as an editor) on one article, the writer sent a message to my managing editor asking for more money and complaining about all the rounds of editing. It turns out she was just as frustrated with me as I was with her. My story is it was all her fault. Her story is it was all mine. To make a long story short, I started to tell myself a story about this writer that was rife with judgment. In my mind, she was a lazy and entitled millennial who thought she was above editing. I'm not going to lie. I got frustrated. I got mad. I dug deeper into my judgments and my story.

Man plans and the universe laughs. While this was going on, I'd been working on my judgments, trying to notice them, and trying to be more neutral in how I perceived others. I was also working on being grateful for some of the more difficult people in my life because they were providing me the opportunity to do this work. Yet this writer slipped right past me. While I was walking around trying to be all Zen about others, I was judging this writer based on some submitted articles and a few email communications. I had a whole story about her in spite of the fact I didn't really know what was causing the issues.

When I finally was able to take a breath and step back, I also realized something else: my judgments about the writer were a projection based on my own insecurities about my abilities as an editor. In spite of my intense focus on judgment and projection, I was enmeshed in a professional situation where I was doing just that, and in the moment I felt totally justified in doing so.

Once I realized this, I was able to start to apply what I understood about judgment and projection. While I'm still a little agitated, I'm better than I was, and I'm working on it. My awareness of the situation and my intention to heal it and stop making judgments is helping me move forward more calmly and constructively.

I was able to identify my judgments and projections as

personal insecurity related to my third chakra (self-esteem issues). From there, I did energy work with my third chakra to help me resolve those judgments and projections, as well as the deep-seated feelings that were associated with them.

Cultivating Forgiveness

However, that's not to say the writer will be allowed to continue to write for that publication. From an entirely objective point of view, her writing did not meet the requirements of the publication for which she was writing so she was not invited to write additional articles. And that's okay – not every opportunity is for every person. But the stories I told myself about her, the judgments I made, and the emotions I harbored as a result are no longer part of my energy either.

Just like every opportunity isn't right for every person, neither is every relationship right for every life. Although spiritually we are all one, there are some relationships that bring too much toxicity into our lives, and we have to step away from them. However, we can do it with love and without judgment. We can step away from harmful, toxic, or abusive relationships (or even those where we just don't click with someone else) and still spiritually love the other person while not allowing them energetic space in our lives. I call this stepping away with love and after a fashion (although not always in the heat of the moment), I can see the gifts this person brought to me and be grateful their actions allowed me a certain experience of myself or gave me valuable insight into my life's contracts and lessons.

You can do the same thing. You don't have to allow toxic relationships energetic space in your life. I'm not saying to squash how you're feeling if someone has frustrated you, upset you, angered you, or triggered other emotions. Allow yourself to feel those emotions but don't wallow in them. When you're ready, you can release the negativity and step away with love and after a fashion, without judgment. To do this, you must practice forgiveness, which is your next tool for awareness and intention.

People often misunderstand forgiveness. Many believe it is about letting someone off the hook for their behavior or forgetting behaviors that have negatively affected you. For many, forgiveness is all about offering absolution to the other person so they can feel better about what they've done. I disagree. We cannot control how another thinks or feels, so we have no say in how our absolution may or may not affect someone else. However, we can control ourselves. Forgiveness, then, is all about us. My forgiveness is about me, and yours is all about you.

Regardless of what someone else does "to" you, only you can choose how you respond, how you feel, what you say, and how you behave. Nobody can make you feel anything, nor can they make you think, say, or do anything. Only you are in control of those things. So, when someone presents your life in a way you perceive as negative, you get to choose how you respond.

Initially, you may feel angry, sad, hurt, betrayed, jealous, or a whole host of other emotions. And that's natural because you are invested in your separation from others—you truly believe in it—and when someone does something "crappy" to you, you probably tend to feel pretty cruddy yourself. However, when you remove yourself a few steps from the situation, you can look at it and see what gifts are there.

And you can choose to be grateful to the other person for providing you with the opportunity to see those gifts. That is forgiveness.

A Real Life Example of Forgiveness

I'll give you an example. A few years ago, I was making a documentary. One of the participants went on a rampage when I chose to do something with the documentary he didn't feel was beneficial to him. He made some threats (physical, legal, and emotional). It was pretty ugly and as a result, I chose not to release the documentary I'd worked so hard on, written, filmed, edited, and paid for. I was devastated. I was angry, betrayed, hurt, and grieving. However, after that all had time to percolate and work its way through me, I turned the documentary into a book. It was the first book I ever published, and since then I've authored about 20 more. It is my life's passion. Without that person's actions, who knows if I ever would have written the first one, which gave me the confidence to write the rest including this one. That person gave me a gift. His behavior launched me towards not only my life's greatest passion, but also to my livelihood today and what I currently feel is my life's purpose.

Is he in my life anymore? Gosh no. He's kind of scary, and I don't want that energy in my life. But not only am I not mad at him, I'm grateful to him. This is forgiveness. I'm certain unless he reads my work and recognizes himself in my words, he has no idea I've forgiven him. And frankly, he probably doesn't care whether I did. My forgiveness has no effect on him. It only affects me.

Forgiveness, then, is letting go of any negative feelings you harbor about something someone else has done and finding and being grateful for the gifts you've received from their actions. It's about choosing to turn a negative experience into a positive life direction. It's about recognizing someone's soul and the Divine hand in your difficulties with others and realizing that, although they may not consciously understand they have done so, on a soul level they loved you enough to give you a precious gift.

Tools for Projections, Judgments, and Forgiveness

To understand your judgments and projections, use the following process.

1. When you become aware of a judgment, write it in your journal and then answer the following questions.
2. Close your eyes and think about that judgment. Where do you feel it in your body? What else do you notice emotionally, physically, or mentally when you concentrate on it? What images come to mind?
3. Is the judgment based on factual information, or is it based on suppositions you are making about the person or situation? If you can't tell, write the facts without any emotional content or narrative. Remove the story you are telling yourself about it and allow yourself to only relate facts.
4. How does the story you're telling yourself about this judgment apply to factors in your own life you don't want to acknowledge? Listen to your intuition and evaluate yourself honestly.
5. What reasons could you have for keeping that judgment? How will it benefit or serve you? What reasons could you have for releasing the judgment? How will releasing it benefit or serve you?

6. How would you feel if you no longer held that judgment? What would it cost you to release? How would you benefit from letting it go?

7. Now, take the thing for which you are judging someone else and apply it to yourself. For example, if your judgment is, "He is so greedy," apply it to yourself instead. Say, "I'm so greedy." Close your eyes and allow that thought to sink in. How does it feel? Does it apply to you in some way? What emotions do you feel? How does it feel in your body? Is it a belief you harbor about yourself but don't want to acknowledge?

8. Once you recognize your judgments and understand how they make you feel and how your judgments towards others might apply to you, set your intention to release it.

9. Close your eyes and picture your judgment as a dark shadow in your body. Now, visualize the dark shadow draining from you and flowing from whatever part of your body is touching the Earth. Allow the judgment to sink into the Earth, which will absorb and neutralize it. Then, imagine light pouring down from above and filling your entire body, including the space where the shadow for the judgment once lived.

10. If you continue to feel negative emotions surrounding the judgment, repeat the above exercise or move on to the work of forgiveness.

Questions for Examination

Forgiveness is entirely up to you. Awareness and intention are the first step towards achieving it. Below are some questions for self-examination to help you work towards forgiveness.

1. Who in your life are you still harboring ill feelings towards?
2. What is the source of those ill feelings? What actions and/or words has the other party used that continue to cause your ill feelings?
3. How has this affected you negatively?
4. How has it affected you positively? Can you see any opportunities or gifts it has presented? What are they? How have they enriched your life?
5. How is harboring the ill feelings towards the other person helping you? How is it hurting you?
6. Does holding on to your anger or hurt benefit you in some way? How?
7. What would it cost you to release those ill feelings? How would you benefit if you did? How do you think you would feel if you let go of the negative feelings you are harboring towards the other person? Can you see ways in which it would help you?

Exercises to Facilitate Forgiveness

Once you've examined your feelings and understood them, it is time to begin the process of letting go. You can try any or all of the following exercises to help facilitate your forgiveness.

- Acknowledge the other person did not cause you pain, nor did their actions cause you pain. It's important you recognize you chose pain in response to what they said or did.
- Visualize the person as a baby or small child before he or she engaged in the actions that precipitated your pain. Can you feel the love for that small child? If so, notice that person today is the same soul that was there when he or she was the small child you are able to love.

- Visualize the other person and notice energetic ties running from them to you as strands of light. Imagine cutting those strands while saying, "I release you."
- Visualize the other person surrounded by light and love. Offer your love and gratitude for their willingness to show up in your life as someone difficult in order to share the gifts you have received from them.
- See the person you need to forgive in your mind's eye. Visualize a green light running from your heart chakra to theirs with light flowing between the two.

Take Positive Steps

While forgiveness can happen in a single moment of choice, more often than not it is a process. Here are some steps to take to help you forgive when you feel hurt by something someone else did.

1. Allow Yourself the Anger and Hurt

It's okay to feel these things in the immediate wake of abuse or betrayal. To quash them and pretend to be happy is being untrue to yourself, so you need to allow these emotions to pass through you. In fact, allowing yourself the full force of the experience helps them to pass more quickly. So in the immediate aftermath of the precipitating incident, do what you've got to do. Yell. Scream. Cry. Talk to a supportive friend about your feelings. Write it all out in your journal. Do what it takes to allow yourself the full force of your emotions.

2. But not for too Long

Give yourself some time, but realize that at some point, the negativity becomes a destructive force – not towards the other person, but in your psyche. After you've allowed the full force of your emotions, start taking tentative steps towards forgiveness.

3. Expect Resistance

It's human nature to want to exact revenge, to want to hold on to your anger and resentment, and to want the object of your anger to feel your wrath. So as you start to explore the concept of forgiveness, expect pushback from your ego in the form of a big "HELL NO." This, too, is natural.

4. Forgive Yourself First

If we're being completely honest, when we are betrayed or hurt by another, we always turn on ourselves at least a little. We seek to blame ourselves for the incident that has arisen. We blame ourselves for feeling angry when we should be positive. We blame ourselves for trusting. Therefore, before you can let go of your anger towards another, you must first let go of your anger towards yourself. Surround yourself with the light of love and treat yourselves kindly.

5. Love Yourself

Since forgiveness is always an act of self-love, it's important to remember as you work your way towards it that you are doing this for you so you can be free and move forward in your life. Forgiveness always starts from a place of self love.

6. Look for the Lessons You've Learned

In every act of betrayal, every time we are hurt, every time we are angered, there is a lesson or opportunity there. So when you're ready, look at the lessons you have learned or opportunities you have received from the acts that require forgiveness. Somewhere in there is a kernel of light for you if you are willing to find it. Once you do, even though it's difficult, experiment with gratitude for the lesson you learned or the positive changes it has brought about in your life.

Chapter 7 – Meditation

Meditation has numerous benefits for the body, mind, emotions, and spirit. Some are even scientifically proven, and some studies show actual physical and mental health benefits from a daily meditation practice. Among the many benefits:

- It is relaxing.
- It calms stress.
- It improves focus and concentration.
- It improves emotional control.
- It can improve your physical health.
- It improves sleep.
- It can spur positive thinking.
- It can heighten intuitive abilities.
- It creates brain changes that provide protection against mental illness.
- It can help you set, clarify, and reach goals.
- It can provide spiritual insight and connect you to your Divine guidance system.
- It can lead to communion with the Divine.
- It can raise your vibration.

Did you see that last one? That's right! It increases your vibration. Not only can you increase your vibration from the act of meditating, but all of the other benefits that come before that last bullet point are also factors that can help raise your vibration. So meditation is super important.

Many people believe meditation takes a big commitment or there's only a set way to do it. However, even five to ten minutes of meditation daily can make a difference. If you can go longer, great. Some days, I get in the groove and go for 30 minutes or longer. Some days, all I've got in me is five minutes. Either way, I don't sweat it, and I don't force it. I just go with what feels intuitively right to me.

For years I swore I couldn't meditate or at least not in the classical sense. I have one of those incredibly active minds that never shuts up. Not only was it my experience my mind was never free of thought, but I usually had multiple layers of thoughts zinging around my brain all at once. Some might suggest I had metaphysical ADD.

When I would try to meditate, it would go a little something like this:

"Ommmmm.....clear my mind. Clear my mind. Check it out! I'm doing it! My mind is actually free from thought! Speaking of thought, I'm thinking about switching over to a low-carb diet. I wonder if bacon is actually considered a healthy food on a low-carb diet? Speaking of bacon, I see there's a special on pork products at the grocery store. I need to go get groceries. Let's see – what do I need? I guess it depends on what I plan to make for dinners this week. Dinner last night was so fun. It was great to see Debbie. I always have such a good time with her. She's the one that suggested I meditate, which is what I'm doing now. Thank goodness I am able to keep my mind so clear and free of thought. Oh. Crap. Ommmmmmm...."

Over the years I had various people in my life suggest I meditate, and I'd try. Oh how I'd try. Unfortunately, instead of feeling peaceful and Zen, I wound up even more frustrated than when I started. Which is why I never thought I'd recommend regular meditation to others. Yet that is exactly what I am doing.

What I've discovered since my time as a frustrated meditator is this: There are many different ways to engage in meditation. If one doesn't work for you, try something else. That's how it eventually clicked for me...I tried various meditation practices. I kept at it. And finally I found one that worked for me and as I gained discipline and focus, I found I was able to engage in other forms, as well.

So while I recommend you meditate daily, I also suggest you don't force it because when we force ourselves to do something we don't want to or are uncomfortable with, we often have negative thoughts and feelings associated with it, which can contribute to energetic disruptions and imbalances. Try any of the following techniques and see what works for you, or come up with your own version of quieting your mind and tuning in to your higher self.

Grounding

Grounding is a form of meditation you can do relatively quickly, but it helps you feel refreshed. It is especially beneficial if you are in a difficult situation and are feeling emotionally, physically, mentally, or spiritually off balance.

When you ground yourself, you connect yourself to the Earth and to your body, which can help you feel more supported and balanced. Grounding helps balance the lower chakras, particularly your root chakra.

Grounding Meditation #1

The first type of grounding meditation is simple. Anyone can do it virtually any time. All you have to do is connect your bare feet to the ground. Some people also call this earthing. I especially like taking off my shoes and running around in the grass, but you can also just walk around your house barefoot. As you do, pay special attention to the connection of the bottom of your feet to the earth. Do it as frequently as you need for as long or short of a period as you wish.

Another form of earthing involves lying on the grass. When I exercise outdoors, I use this form of grounding under the guise of "stretching." And I do stretch for a moment or two, but my ultimate goal is always to lie down on the grass and look up at the sky. It connects me to the earth and makes me feel peaceful and happy.

Grounding Meditation #2

This next meditation is almost as quick, and it doesn't involve going outside or taking off your shoes, so it's a great grounding meditation to do at the office or in a social situation.

1. Sit on a chair with your feet flat on the ground, or sit directly on the floor.
2. Close your eyes and imagine roots growing from whichever part of you is touching the floor and extending deeply into the earth. Do this as quickly or for as long as you wish.

Grounding Meditation #3

Your hara, which is located just about in the center of your abdomen, is your center of balance. It is believed by many to be the point that serves as a gateway to the Earth.

1. For this meditation, sit on the floor or in a chair with your feet flat on the ground.
2. Close your eyes and breathe deeply.
3. Place both hands over your hara and imagine roots extending down from your hara and into the earth.
4. Visualize the roots extending all the way to the center of the earth, which is filled with a ball of pink, glowing light.
5. Wrap your roots around the glowing pink light and visualize the light moving up the roots and

into your hara. Feel the pink light as a gentle warmth growing under your hands and filling your abdomen.

Traditional Meditation

Traditional Eastern meditation is the type most people consider "real" meditation (although any activity can be meditative if you allow yourself to focus). Typically, it involves sitting comfortably on the floor or on a cushion in the lotus position, closing your eyes, and clearing your mind. As thoughts drift into your mind during this type of meditation, you notice them but gently release them instead of investing or following the thoughts. The chalkboard exercise mentioned in a previous chapter is one technique for clearing your mind (visualize your thoughts as words on a chalkboard and then see them being erased).

A few other techniques for noticing and clearing thoughts during meditation include:

- As thoughts arise, see them as balloons. Say, "release' and watch the balloons drift away.
- Visualize an empty void. As thoughts drift in, watch them dissolve.

Mantra Meditation

In mantra meditation, you focus your mind by chanting a mantra and focusing solely on that mantra. If your mind wanders, gently bring it back to your mantra. Traditional Eastern meditation practices focus on mantras such as Om (pronounced "aum"), which is a sacred Hindu mantra that represents the universe. Other traditional Eastern mantras include:

- Om mani padme hum, which literally means the jewel in the lotus, which is an invocation of the compassion of the Buddha
- Om shanti shanti shanti, which is an invocation of peace
- Ham-sah, which means "I am that"

However, it isn't necessary for you to repeat ancient Eastern mantras. You can use anything that has meaning to you. It can be an affirmation, a statement of love, or a statement of purpose. Some suggested mantras include:

- I am that I am
- Peace
- Compassion
- Love
- Joy
- By changing my thoughts, I change the world
- I am enough
- I am living my purpose
- I am connected to the Divine

These are just a few of many. Choose one that has meaning for you.

Many meditators who chant mantras use prayer beads to count their mantras. They do this by touching one bead at a time for each time they speak the mantra. There are many types of prayer beads available to you. You can use Buddhist malas made of gemstones, lotus seeds, or precious woods; Catholic rosaries; Anglican prayer beads; or any strand of beads that has meaning and significance for you. Holding the beads and counting your mantras with them is another excellent way to focus your mind as you meditate.

Focus Meditation

Focus meditation involves providing some type of a

sensory input that you can focus on as you meditate to keep your mind quiet and focused. There are a number of different methods. Some are listed below, but feel free to come up with your own ways of focusing, as well.

Gassho

Dr. Mikao Usui taught the Gassho meditation method to his Reiki students as a means of focusing. Gassho is simple to do.

1. Hold your hands in prayer position with your fingertips touching either in front of your heart or in your lap as you sit with your eyes closed.
2. Clear your mind, breathe deeply, and focus all your attention on the point where the tips of your two middle fingers touch.
3. If your mind wanders, gently bring it back to the sensation of your two middle fingers touching.

Visual Focus Meditation

This type of meditation uses visual stimulus and a soft gaze to keep your mind focused. While you can use anything as a point of visual focus, many people use a flickering candle or a crystal of some type. During this meditation, set the object six to 12 inches in front of you and gaze at it with a soft gaze as you breathe deeply. If your mind wanders, gently bring it back to your visual focus point.

Auditory Focus Meditation

Again, there are numerous techniques for auditory focus meditation. One involves placing your hands on your chest and humming a tune. Focus on both the humming and sound of the tune as well as how it feels in your chest as you hum it. You can also focus on any sound, such as a relaxing piece of music, the sound of birds singing, waves crashing on a beach, or any other sound that has meaning for you. If your mind wanders, gently bring it back to your focus point.

Color Focus Meditation

Color focus meditation is a mental focusing technique that works very well for people who think in pictures or are able to visualize. To do a color focus meditation:

1. Close your eyes and focus on your third eye as if there is a movie screen on the inside of your forehead.
2. On that screen, visualize any color you like. Focus on that color.
3. When you feel your mind start to wander, focus on a new color and gently bring your mind back to your focus.

Touch Focus Meditation Technique

You can also use touch as a meditation focus technique. Try this easy focus meditation any time you have a few minutes to be in a meditative state, or for longer full-length meditation sessions.

1. Tap your forefinger against some part of exposed skin on your body. It could be the tip of your nose, a cheek, the tip of your thumb, or anywhere else.
2. Focus completely on where your finger is touching your body. Notice how it feels when the finger taps, as well as how it feels in the space between the taps.
3. Vary the speed and pressure of the tapping. Tap slowly for a few minutes, and then speed it up. How slowly can you tap? How quickly? Try a very light pressure and a heavier pressure. Lift your finger farther away in the space between the tap or keep it very close to the skin.

4. As you tap, notice the friction. Notice the energy between the finger and your skin, and notice how that energy or friction changes with your different distances, speeds, and pressures of tapping.
5. Do this for as long as you like. If thoughts come into your mind, gently return your focus to your tapping.

Breathing Meditation

To perform breathing meditation, close your eyes and focus on your breath. If your mind wanders, gently bring your attention back to your breath. There are variations on this.

- You can breathe naturally and focus on that.
- Practice alternate nostril breathing (a yoga technique). Close your right nostril and take a deep breath in through your left. Unplug the right nostril and plug the left and breathe out through the right nostril. With your left nostril still plugged, breathe in through your right nostril. Unplug your left nostril and breathe out through it. Continue rotating in this manner, focusing on your breathing.
- Breathe in for a count of six and breathe out for a count of six. Focus on the spaces between when you breathe in and breathe out, noticing when the breath turns over.

Movement Meditation

Movement meditation involves clearing your mind as you focus on whatever movement your body makes, and if your mind wanders, you gently draw it back to the movement. Some movement activities that are excellent for this type of meditation include:

- Walking a labyrinth

- Walking outdoors in nature
- Dancing
- Yoga
- Tai chi

Prayer

Prayer is another form of meditation that is highly personal. I'm not going to tell you that you should pray or how you should do it, because you need to pray in a way that is meaningful to you. To make your prayer more meditative, focus fully on it. It can be a prayer you already know, such as the Lord's Prayer or a Psalm, a piece of meaningful poetry, or you can pray about whatever is in your heart.

Guided Meditation

In guided meditation, the focus point to help you clear your mind is using a recording of someone guiding you through a meditation. You can find many of these online, as smartphone apps, and elsewhere for free or very low cost. Guided meditations have many focuses, such as clearing chakras or opening your heart. Find a meditation that has meaning for you. As you listen, focus on the words and sounds and allow your mind to visualize what you are hearing.

Chakra Meditation

Chakra meditation involves visualizing each of your chakras and imagining energy flowing through it. It is an especially good way of balancing your chakras during meditation. To perform a chakra meditation, do the following:

1. Close your eyes and breathe deeply.
2. Focus on your root chakra. Imagine it as a disc of red light swirling in either a clockwise or counter clockwise direction. Notice if energy can move through the chakra or if it is blocked.

If it is blocked, visualize the chakra opening and white light flowing through the red, moving up into your sacral chakra.

3. Visualize your sacral chakra as a swirling disc of orange light. See the white light energy moving through the chakra and up into your solar plexus.

4. Visualize your solar plexus as a rotating disc of glowing yellow or golden light. Move the white light up through the solar plexus chakra and into the heart.

5. Visualize your heart chakra as a rotating disc of glowing green light. Visualize the light moving up through the heart chakra and into your throat.

6. Visualize your throat chakra as a spinning disc of glowing blue light. Move the white light energy up through the throat chakra and into the third eye.

7. Visualize your third eye chakra as a spinning disc of violet light. Move the white light up through your third eye chakra and into your crown chakra.

8. Visualize your crown chakra as a spinning disc of glowing white light. Visualize the white light flowing up through the chakra and into the heavens.

9. Now, visualize the white light coming down from the heavens and moving through each chakra and into the Earth.

Root Chakra Meditation

1. Sit on the ground in a comfortable position with your eyes closed and breathe deeply. If you wish, hold your hands in the mudra (see movement chapter) for the first chakra. Alternatively, you can gently place your hands over your root chakra (in your lap) and visualize

healing light flowing from the universe into your hands and out through your hands into the chakra.

2. With each breath, imagine red energy flowing up from the earth and into your root chakra.
3. Each inhale, visualize the red ball growing in your root chakra and filling the area.
4. As the ball grows, repeat the following mantras (as many or as few as you'd like):
   - I am safe.
   - I am secure.
   - I am firmly rooted to the Earth.
   - I am connected to all of life.
   - I heal my childhood wounds
   - I am grateful for the blessings from my family.
5. Sit with the glowing red ball for as long as you like. When you are finished, express your gratitude to the universe.

Sacral Chakra Meditation

1. Sit comfortably on the ground or in a chair with your feet rooted firmly on the ground. Breathe deeply. If you wish, hold your hands in the second chakra mudra (see movement chapter). Alternatively, you can rest your hands gently over your sacral chakra and visualize healing light flowing from the universe through your hands and into the sacral chakra.
2. As you breathe, visualize a ball of orange light starting to grow in your naval region. Allow each breath to expand the light and feel its warmth as it does.
3. As the ball grows, repeat the one, some, or all of the following mantras on your exhale:
   - Everyone one I meet helps me grow spiritually.
   - I am grateful for my creativity.
   - I release my need for control.
   - I bring my creative ideas to expression.
   - I keep my word to myself and others.
   - I am grateful for prosperity in my life.

- I choose from love and not from fear.
- The universe meets all of my needs as they arise.

4. Sit with the glowing orange ball for as long as you like. When you are finished, express your gratitude to the universe.

Solar Plexus Chakra Meditation #1

1. Sit comfortably on the ground or in a chair with your feet rooted firmly on the ground, or lie on your back on the floor or a comfortable cushion. Breathe deeply. If you wish, hold your hands in the third chakra mudra (see movement chapter). Alternatively, you can rest your hands gently over your solar plexus chakra and visualize healing light flowing from the universe through your hands and into the chakra.

2. As you breathe, visualize a ball of golden light starting to grow in your solar plexus region. Allow each breath to expand the light and feel its warmth as it does.

3. Visualize the golden light from your solar plexus flowing outside of you, around you, and through you as you notice a sense of well-being and self worth surrounding you.

4. As the golden light surrounds you, repeat the one, some, or all of the following mantras on your exhale:
   - I love myself.
   - I offer great worth to the universe.
   - I am responsible for my own life.
   - I make choices that support my well being.
   - I like and approve of myself and in doing so, do not need the approval of others.

5. Sit with the glowing golden ball for as long as you like. When you are finished, express your gratitude to the universe.

Solar Plexus Chakra Meditation #2

1. Sit or lie comfortably and breathe deeply.

2. Imagine a golden yellow beam of light coming from the universe and into your solar plexus chakra.
3. Visualize feelings of self love and self worth entering your chakra through that beam of light and spreading throughout your entire body. Visualize those feelings filling every cell.

Heart Chakra Meditation #1

1. Sit comfortably on the ground or in a chair with your feet rooted firmly on the ground, or lie on your back on the floor or a comfortable cushion. Breathe deeply. If you wish, hold your hands in the heart chakra mudra (see movement chapter). Alternatively, you can rest your hands gently over your heart chakra and visualize healing light flowing from the universe through your hands and into the chakra.
2. As you breathe, visualize a ball of warm green light starting to grow in your heart region. Allow each breath to expand the light and feel its warmth as it does. Picture the green light as love, filling your entire body and expanding into every cell.
3. As the green light surrounds you, repeat one, some, or all of the following mantras on your exhale:
    - I am filled with the love of the universe.
    - I am unconditionally loved.
    - I love unconditionally.
    - I am compassionate.
    - The universe has infinite compassion for me.
    - I heal my relationships with love.
4. Sit with the green ball for as long as you like. When you are finished, express your gratitude to the universe.

Heart Chakra Meditation #2 – Meditation for Forgiveness

1. Sit or lie comfortably with your eyes closed and breathe deeply with your hands at your side or in your lap.
2. In your mind's eye, as you breathe visualize a person whom you need forgiveness from, or who you need to forgive.

3. Now, visualize a beam of green light flowing from your heart chakra to theirs. Feel the connection of unconditional love and compassion flowing across the beam of light between your two heart chakras. Remain in this meditation for as long as you need.

Heart Chakra Meditation #3 – Healing with Love

1. Sit or lie comfortably with your eyes closed with your hands at your side or in your lap and breathe deeply.
2. Visualize for a moment what it is that needs healing. It could be your own hurt feelings, it could be a relationship, it could be a situation, or something else.
3. Now, visualize moving that which needs healing into your heart and surrounding it with love and the glowing green light from your heart chakra. As you visualize this, focus on the beating of your heart.
4. See the green light flowing through your beating heart, and with every heartbeat, the love flows throughout your body.
5. Now imagine the green light and love flowing not only through you but out of you, surrounding you.
6. Do this for as long as it takes for you to feel peace.

Throat Chakra Meditation #1

1. Sit comfortably on the ground or in a chair with your feet rooted firmly on the ground, or lie on your back on the floor or a comfortable cushion. Breathe deeply. If you wish, hold your hands in the throat chakra mudra (see movement chapter). Alternatively, you can rest your hands gently over your throat chakra and visualize healing light flowing from the universe through your hands and into the chakra.
2. As you breathe, visualize a ball of warm blue light starting to grow in your throat region. Allow each breath to expand the light and feel its warmth as it does.
3. As the blue light surrounds you, repeat one, some, or all of the following mantras on your exhale:

- I speak my truth.
- I give expression to my creative ideas.
- I listen when others speak.
- I trust in the Divine.
- I am open to receive Divine guidance.
- I am grateful for my willpower.
- I act upon Divine guidance.

4. Sit with the blue light for as long as you like. When you are finished, express your gratitude to the universe.

Throat Chakra Meditation #2

1. Sit or lie comfortably with your hands in your lap or at your side. Close your eyes and breathe deeply through your nose.
2. Exhale through your mouth forcefully. As you do, use your voice to express the breath, saying, "Haaaaaa" as you exhale. Feel the vibration in your chest and throat as you sound your voice.
3. Do this for as long as you wish.

Third Eye Chakra Meditation #1

1. Sit comfortably on the ground or in a chair with your feet rooted firmly on the ground, or lie on your back on the floor or a comfortable cushion. Breathe deeply. If you wish, hold your hands in the third eye chakra mudra (see movement chapter). Alternatively, you can rest one hand gently over the third eye chakra and visualize healing light flowing from the universe through your hand and into the chakra.
5. As you breathe, visualize a ball of violet light starting to grow in the middle of your forehead. Allow each breath to expand the light and feel its warmth as it does.
6. As the violet light surrounds you, repeat one, some, or all of the following mantras on your exhale:
   - I listen to my intuition.
   - I act on my intuition.
   - I am changing what I need to change.

- My higher self communicates me through my intuition and I am open to its messages.
- I am grateful for Divine guidance.
7. Sit with the violet light for as long as you like. When you are finished, express your gratitude to the universe.

Third Eye Chakra Meditation #2

1. Sit or lie comfortably with your hands in your lap or at your sides and breathe deeply.
2. Focus your inner vision on the inside of your forehead where your third eye is. This will act as a sort of movie screen.
3. Watch the images that arise in your mind's eye as you maintain focus. Do not judge or evaluate the images or hold on to them. Instead, just watch as they arise, shift, and change.
4. Continue for as long as you like.

Third Eye Chakra Meditation #3

1. Sit or lie comfortably with your hands in your lap or at your sides and breathe deeply.
2. Visualize your pineal gland as a glowing globe in the center of your brain.
3. Imagine your pineal gland begins to glow and emit light.
4. Allow the light from your pineal gland to fill your head, and then move throughout your body.
5. Finally, allow the light from the pineal gland to spread out into the space around you as you bask in the glow. Do this for as long as you wish.

Crown Chakra Meditation #1

1. Sit comfortably on the ground or in a chair with your feet rooted firmly on the ground. Breathe deeply. If you wish, hold your hands in the crown chakra mudra (see movement chapter). Alternatively, you can rest one hand gently over the crown chakra and visualize healing light flowing from the universe through your hand and into the chakra.

2. As you breathe, visualize a ball of white light starting to grow in the middle of your crown. Allow each breath to expand the light and feel its warmth as it does.

3. As the white light surrounds you, repeat one, some, or all of the following mantras on your exhale:
   - I am a piece of the Divine.
   - Divinity is in me.
   - I am one with the Universe.
   - I am one with all that is.
   - I am.

4. Sit with the white light for as long as you like. When you are finished, express your gratitude to the universe.

Crown Chakra Meditation #2

1. Sit or lie comfortably with your eyes closed and your hands by your side or in your lap. Breathe deeply.

2. Imagine you are on a footpath winding through nature. Notice your feet on the path. Begin to walk along the path and notice you are moving up hill.

3. As you travel up hill, imagine you come to a pool of glowing red energy. Walk through the pool and feel its energy, and then continue upward along the path.

4. Imagine you next come to a pool of glowing orange energy. Walk through the pool allowing it to wash over you, and then continue upward along the path.

5. Imagine you next come to a pool of glowing golden energy. Walk through the pool, allowing it to wash over you, and then continue upward along the path.

6. Imagine next you come to a pool of glowing green energy. Walk through the pool allowing it to wash over you, and then continue upward along the path.

7. Imagine next you come to a pool of glowing blue energy. Walk through the pool allowing it to wash over you, and then continue upward along the path.

8. Imagine you next come to a pool of glowing violet energy. Walk through the pool allowing the energy to wash over you.

9. As you step out of the violet pool, notice the path has become very steep. Look up and notice the top of the path is obscured by white, fluffy clouds.
10. Walk upward along the path and into the clouds. As you reach the top, the clouds clear and a brilliant white light shines down from above surrounding you. The light is warm, loving, and safe. You are standing on a plateau at the top of a mountain, and below you see the path you just traveled with its glowing pools of energy. Turn from the edge of the plateau and notice a beautiful white temple with a grand set of steps leading up to it. In front of the temple is a glowing pool of white light.
11. Step into the pool and allow yourself to fully immerse in the white light. As you step out, walk up the steps and open the door of the temple to step inside.
12. The temple is filled with an even more brilliant white light than you experienced outside. You may hear the sounds of a glorious choir, and you know you are surrounded by love. In this beautiful room you see a beam of even more brilliant white light shining like a spotlight with the comfiest chair you can imagine in the center. Go sit in the chair and relax, allowing the brilliant white light to shine down on you and heal you for as long as you like.
13. When you are done, give thanks and then retrace your steps out of the temple and down the mountain to the start of your path.

Affirmation and Visualization

Affirmations and visualization are one of the first types of meditation I felt I was really adept at. They are both powerful tools in raising your vibrational frequency and bringing positive changes into your life. To use affirmation:

1. Come up with a list of about five positive messages you want to send to yourself. They can be about who you choose to be (such as, "I

recognize the presence of the Divine inside of me"), something you want to do (such as, "I earn my living serving my Divine purpose in the universe"), something you'd like to make manifest in your health (such as, "Every cell in my body vibrates with optimal health"), or something you'd like to have more of in your life (such as, "I give thanks for the abundance and prosperity flowing into my life").

2. Create affirmations you can remember, that are specific, and that are stated in the positive as if you already have what you want. Instead of saying, "I want," say, "I am," "I have," "Or I give thanks for," and then make a positive statement of what that is.

3. Repeat your affirmations daily. Do it in meditation, write them several times in your journal, or speak them aloud (this is especially powerful if you do it when looking into your eyes in the mirror).

4. You may also want to keep your affirmations with you so you can remember them throughout the day as you feel you need.

Visualization is essentially affirmation without the words, using pictures instead. Imagine what your life would look like if you were living exactly as you wish, and then visualize yourself living that life. Sit with your eyes closed breathing deeply and visualize. Notice how you look and how you feel as you live in this life you have created for yourself in your visualization. When you are done, give thanks to the universe for making it so.

Enhancing Affirmations with Neuro Linguistic Programming (NLP)

Neuro linguistic programming is a technique you can use to help change the way you think, something that is very valuable in vibrational healing given thoughts have energy that can manifest physically. While there are many techniques in NLP that make it worthwhile for you to dig into more deeply on your own, the one that I want to discuss here is the association of hand gestures with a positive thought in order to set that thought more deeply. This technique is called anchoring. For our purposes, we're going to use anchoring to deepen your affirmations. Here's how you do it.

1. State your affirmation and truly allow yourself to feel how you will feel when you have achieved that which you are affirming. Will you feel joyful? Powerful? What will your emotions be? What will your life look like? As you visualize this, allow the emotions to well up deeply inside of you.
2. When you get to this state of deep emotion and gratitude, create a gesture. For example, you can create an "OK" sign with your thumb and forefinger or tap twice on the side of your nose with a forefinger. Try to make the gesture unique and not something you would normally do.
3. Do this a few times over the next few days, always using the exact same gesture.
4. Moving forward, you can reset the affirmation throughout your day without speaking or thinking of it simply by repeating the gesture. When you do, the feelings you had during the initial step should come back to you. This helps to reinforce your daily affirmation practice. Cool, huh?

Five Things that Can Lower the Effectiveness of Your Affirmations

If you want your affirmations to work, you need to speak, write, or think them once a day. That's a good start, but there more to it than that. Let's take a look at some of the things that may serve as roadblocks to affirmations.

1. Continuing to think negatively

You've probably heard the old axe, "Thoughts become things." This is true whether you are consciously making positive statements and affirmations, or if you continuously have negative words flit through your mind without giving them much of a thought at all.

Whether you know it or not, you're constantly sending affirmations out into the universe, even when you're not making a conscious effort to do so. For example, every time you say, "I'm so broke," or, "I can never catch a break," you're sending a specific request into the universe, which has no choice but to respond.

These subconscious or barely conscious thoughts and statements are just as powerful as consciously spoken, written, or thought affirmations. In some cases, they may be even more powerful because they become the running dialogue you have with yourself without even thinking about it.

So what's the solution? It's important to monitor your thoughts and catch yourself thinking negative things when they arise. Every time you catch yourself thinking a negative thought, stop immediately and say in your head or aloud, "Cancel that....I am....." and make a positive statement instead. For example, if you catch yourself thinking, "I am always broke," immediately think or say, "Cancel that. I have all the money I need to live the life I desire."

2. Doing your affirmations only once a day

Affirmations are an active process, and they require concentrated effort to overcome the volume of negative thoughts you are thinking. I believe in active affirmation, or using affirmations not only as a meditative ritual once or twice a day, but also using them throughout the day as negative thoughts arise.

Let's look at an example. Say you want to lose weight, but every time you put on clothing, catch a glimpse of yourself in the mirror, or eat something you know isn't conducive to weight loss, you think something like, "I'm so fat," "I'm never going to lose weight," or, "even if I do lose weight, I'm just going to gain it back." Even if once a day, you're closing your eyes and uttering with conviction, "I am losing weight," or "I am thin and healthy," the sheer volume of your negative thoughts about being overweight will outweigh the once per day you think or speak your affirmation.

The solution here is the same as the previous one. Monitor your thoughts, catch negativity, and immediately cancel it out with a positive statement. You can also take a few moments several times a day to re-set your affirmations in your mind. For example, you can carry them in a document on your smartphone and read them whenever you have a break.

3. Making statements of want or need

The combination of the word "I" plus whatever statement you make about it afterward, such as "I want," "I am," or "I need," is a very powerful combination, and the universe responds in kind. So, if you say to yourself, "I want more money," the universe will very literally give you what you just said – the experience of wanting more money. Likewise, if your affirmation is, "I need to find a significant other," the universe will give you the experience of needing a significant other.

What should you do instead? Remember the combination of I plus the second word is powerfully creative. Instead of saying, "I want," or "I need," make a statement as if you already have that which you desire. Let's look at the significant other affirmation as an example. Instead of saying, "I need to find a significant other," use the affirmation, "I am in a loving and joyful relationship with my significant other." While this may not be true at the moment, know that the universe has already set the wheels in motion.

4. Failing to express gratitude

I make gratitude part of my affirmations, because it strengthens them and is an important component of what I like to call *acting as if*. When you act as if you already have that which you desire, including thanking the universe for something, it strengthens the power of the affirmation. Therefore, all of my affirmations either start or end with gratitude. For example, you might want to say, "I am grateful I am in vibrant health," if your affirmation is about your health and well-being.

5. Not visualizing

Visualization is another tool that combines powerfully with affirmation. Visualization helps you see and experience yourself after you've achieved what it is you desire. I recommend closing your eyes for a five-minute visualization session as part of your meditation after you've done your affirmations. When visualizing, try to picture yourself already having achieved that which you seek, and allow yourself to bask in the emotions of how it would feel to be, do, or have those things.

There is no magic to affirmations. It's about setting intention and maintaining focus on that which you choose while expressing gratitude to the universe for providing it. Thoughts are creative, and focusing them more carefully can help shorten the time between when you put something out in the universe and when you receive it.

Gratitude

I'm including gratitude in the meditation chapter, but the truth is you can include gratitude in any and all of your practices. For me, gratitude is a daily practice in which I engage. Gratitude helps raise your vibration by focusing you on the positive aspects of your existence.

I try to begin and end each day with gratitude and sprinkle it throughout. When I wake up, I list what I'm grateful for. I often drift off to sleep at night giving thanks for the things I am grateful for, as well. Throughout the day, I try to express my gratitude. There are many opportunities in every moment to express gratitude. Here are a few:

- When you go somewhere and arrive safely and efficiently
- Before and after you eat to the food sources (plant and animal) that have sacrificed their lives to nourish you
- To people who treat you kindly
- To your body after exercise for supporting you and carrying you
- To your home for providing you comfort and shelter
- Whenever anything positive happens

- Whenever anything negative happens to provide you an opportunity to explore some aspect of yourself
- To people in your life who treat you unkindly and allow you to uncover another layer that needs healing

Gratitude Meditation

You can also make gratitude a meditation practice. Do the following:

1. Sit or lie comfortably with your eyes closed, breathing deeply. Place your hands gently over your heart chakra.
2. Think of something you are grateful for. Make it a big something you are grateful for, such as a partner, children, or a life's passion. Allow yourself to truly feel the magnitude of your gratitude in that moment.
3. Now, bring that feeling of gratitude into your heart chakra. Feel it growing underneath your hands. When it feels too big to be contained within the walls of your chest, move your hands to your lap or sides and allow the gratitude to pulse through your body with your heartbeat and out of your body into the space surrounding you.
4. See how far you can project the gratitude into the world and universe. Allow it to continue to grow as you meditate.
5. When you are ready, take three deep breaths, slowly return to your body, and open your eyes.

Other Activities as Meditation

You can make any activity into a meditative one if you give it your full focus. For example, I make jewelry, and I find it a very meditative practice. My mind clears, and I focus completely on what I'm doing. If you have a hobby, art, or craft, they provide an opportunity for meditation if you focus on what you are doing and let all thoughts fall by the wayside. Some activities that may work for you include:

- Fiber arts, such as crochet, sewing, quilting knitting, or needlework
- Coloring
- Photography
- Painting
- Cooking
- Writing or journaling
- Being out in nature

Meditation Is What You Choose It to Be

Meditation is a powerful tool for raising your vibration, and it doesn't have to be uncomfortable or difficult. Whether it's listing things you're grateful for as you drift off to sleep, engaging in movement, sitting quietly and clearing your mind, or getting immersed in a favorite art or hobby, making meditative experiences a regular part of life can help you clear energetic imbalances and tune in to guidance from higher realms.

Chapter 8 – Harnessing the Power of Dreams

Everyone dreams, although many people believe they don't. Dreams are an important vibrational tool. They are part of your Divine guidance system. In a dream state, you are more open and susceptible to ideas, creative thoughts, and suggestions from your higher self, guides, and the Divine. And when you are able to listen to and interpret Divine guidance, you can raise your own vibration, bring about personal healing, and follow the path of your highest and greatest good.

Not all dreams are Divinely inspired, and not all dreams have messages for you, but many do. Some dreams are simply your mind recapitulating and processing what has happened during your day, but others have great vibrational and spiritual significance.

Symbolic Dreams

Symbolic dreams come directly from your Divine guidance system. These are dreams that often seem to make little sense in the waking world, but once you understand the context of the dream and the symbols it contains, you can decode it and receive a message from your Divine guidance system. In general, symbolic dreams happen regardless of any input from you. In other words, you don't need to ask for a dream or have any intention for the dream to take place. These are the dreams you have many nights and without interpretation, you may have difficulty understanding them. Think of them as unsolicited (but usually good) advice from higher realms.

Lucid Dreams

In lucid dreams (also called conscious dreams), you control the action because you recognize within the dream you are in a dream state and then begin to make choices and have conscious control of what is happening. These types of dreams can be a powerful vibrational healing tool because in the dream you can ask for guidance, seek creative ideas, and more.

Lucid dreaming is a skill that starts with intention. If you'd like to try your hand at it, set the intention before you go to sleep you will have a lucid dream and will be able to remember it the next morning. Then, when you become aware you are dreaming, start to see what you can affect in the dream. Make a choice and see if the dream responds. Start with simple choices (do I turn right or left? Do I sit or stand?) and once you are able to control those very simple aspects, start making larger choices and having the intention to discover things within your dream that will help raise your vibration. The more you practice, the better you will get.

If the first few times you ask you don't seem to have the ability to lucid dream, simply keep setting your intention every night before you go to sleep. You can also ask your higher self and the rest of your Divine guidance system to assist you in this process.

Visitation Dreams

In visitation dreams, loved ones who have died come back and visit you in the dream state. These truly are visitations from those on the other side of the veil, and your visitors may also include spirit guides, your higher self, or others. All come to impart guidance, wisdom, love, and comfort that can help you heal vibrationally. The way to recognize these dreams is through their hyperreal quality. In general, these dreams seem even more real than your waking life.

While visitation dreams typically occur unasked for, you can try setting your intention before you go to sleep that someone (be specific) will visit you. It may take a few days of setting this intention. You may also wish to attune yourself to that person's vibration before you go to sleep. You can do this by looking at photographs, visualizing the person, holding something that belonged to him or her, or recalling fond memories as you drift off to sleep.

You can also try to combine visitation dreams with lucid dreaming so when you are with that person, you can get the most out of the experience. Do this by setting the intention to have a lucid visitation with that person before you go to sleep and setting your intention you will remember the dream the next day. However, don't try to control the dream too much, or you may miss the important information the person visiting you has come to impart. It's important you listen and allow in these types of dreams.

Out of Body Experiences (OBE) or Traveling Dreams

In OBE dreams, a part of your consciousness leaves your body and is free to travel around the universe or interact with other travelers or spirits from other realms. These dreams can occur within the context of a lucid dream (that is, you can control what you do, who you see, and where you travel), or you may notice you have little control over what happens in the dream and you are just going along for the ride. Like visitation dreams, they may be hyper real, and they can often leave you with a sense of ineffability (that is, they are really hard to explain to someone else).

In the case of a lucid OBE, you have the opportunity to create experiences for yourself, talk to important guides, and seek information that will help guide you in your quest for your highest and greatest good. In cases where you notice little control, your higher self or Divine guidance system may be in control. That doesn't make those dreams any less powerful, however. In fact, these dreams may be even more powerful tools because your Divine guidance system has a direct pipeline to your subconscious so they can supply the information you need when you are at your most open to receiving it. You can set the intention to travel as you drift off to sleep.

It is important you dispel any fear you have of the process. One good way to start doing this is to play with having your consciousness leave your body as you drift off to sleep. Set your intention to do this and then notice, for instance, if your consciousness leaves your body even for a moment. Start with hovering over your body for a minute or two and then returning to it. As you grow more skillful and confident, try traveling a little farther for a little longer, but returning as soon as you feel any discomfort. By gradually increasing the time and distance of your travel, you will begin to trust you can return to your body whenever you choose and then you can travel without fear.

Psychic Dreams

Psychic dreams have a similar feeling to visitation dreams. They often have a sense hyper reality and ineffability. You may find they are difficult to explain to others or remember in a linear fashion in your waking life because these types of dreams occur outside of 3-dimensional space and are, instead, occurring in the eternal moment of now that is present in the non-physical realms.

Psychic dreaming typically occurs because you have asked for it, and the dream provides answers to a question you have asked to have answered during the dream. These dreams may be highly symbolic in nature, much like symbolic dreams, and you may need to do some interpreting to understand how the dream answers your question.

To have a psychic dream, ask a question before you go to sleep and set the intention to have the answer come to you in a dream. Always be sure to set the intention you will remember the dream upon waking.

Prophetic Dreams

It's often difficult to distinguish a prophetic dream from a symbolic dream when they occur, although in hindsight you will be able to recognize the difference. This is because you will realize your dream was prophetic after the event you are dreaming about occurs. Prophetic dreams can feel frustrating, especially if they are nonspecific or you don't realize the dreams are predicting something until after the fact, so you are unable to do anything about what the dream is prophesizing. However, prophetic dreams do have their own feel and vibration, so after you learn to recognize how these dreams present for you, there is something you can do about them: you can send generalized vibrational healing to the situation, humanity, or the planet before the incident occurs.

For example, I have prophetic dreams about earthquakes and school shootings. Unfortunately, the details aren't specific enough for me to warn anyone or act on them in any physical way, so I only know after the fact which incident the dream was foretelling. However, I can use these dreams as a vibrational healing tool because when I have them, I can work on sending general vibrational healing to the planet and its inhabitants. Likewise, prophetic dreams only foretell of one probability and if enough people receive them and act upon them by sending vibrational healing to the planet, it may be sufficient to heal the situation before it arises so a different probability occurs.

It's important to note prophetic dreams are not always negative. You can also dream about positive events and send vibrational healing in order to help make that probability a reality in 3-dimensional space.

Recurring Dreams

Many people have recurring dreams. These dreams may be the exact same dream, or they may have a recurring theme. For instance, there was a period in my life where I had two types of dreams about control: one type of dream involved getting in an elevator and the elevator stopping on every floor but mine, and the other involved driving in a car that was rolling down the hill towards a lake, but the brakes weren't working. Both of those dreams were thematically indicating to me I felt out of control over some aspect of my life, and they didn't stop until I'd resolved the issue and felt more in control.

Recurring dreams come without bidding, and they often point you to issues in your life you need to resolve. For example, many people have a dream of returning to their high school and having a test they haven't studied for. While this is a dream sometimes associated with generalized anxiety, it can also be a dream that is telling you that you recently had an opportunity to learn an important karmic lesson, but you chose not to, or it may suggest you pay attention because important lessons are forthcoming.

Pay attention to your recurring dreams. Make note of what has been happening in your life around the time they occur and see if you can discover what the dream is telling you. If you are unable to arrive at a personal interpretation, then try the dream interpretation process presented later in this chapter.

Nightmares

Everyone has nightmares from time to time. While they can be terrifying, nightmares are really just another form of a symbolic dream, although their scary and negative themes may be alerting you to some negative pattern in your life you need to pay attention to and resolve.

You can use the dream interpretation process offered later in this chapter to help you understand what your nightmares mean, and then you can work vibrationally to attempt to heal the issues using other tools in the toolbox.

Remembering Your Dreams

In order for your dreams to serve you as a vibrational healing tool, you must first be able to remember them. Many dreams are ephemeral and slip away quickly once you wake up and start going about your day. However, it is possible to greatly increase the odds of remembering your dreams by taking the following steps.

1. Before you go to sleep each night, set your intention to remember your dreams. Use an affirmation, such as, "As I sleep I dream, and when I wake I will remember all of my dreams."
2. Keep a dream journal, a pad of paper, or a small digital recorder next to your bed. When you awaken, write down your dream or record it on the voice recorder

before you do anything else. List every detail possible from your dreams, because the more details you have, the better you will be able to interpret them. Nothing in dreams is unimportant, so get all of the details before you start your day. Note what you wore, how you felt, background colors, numbers, moods, people, what people wore, hair color and length, facial hair, other unusual identifiers (such as tattoos, etc.), age, behaviors, etc.

3. After you've written down your dreams (or recorded them) from the night before. Offer gratitude to your Divine guidance system for the information and offer gratitude you were able to remember the dream.

Basic Dream Interpretation

Before you start to interpret a dream, ask yourself if it made sense without any symbols in it. For instance, if you dreamed you went to the doctor and he said you had an illness in your kidneys, that may be what the dream was telling you: you need to get your kidneys checked. While dreams can sometimes be that simple and straightforward, often they aren't. In that case, you need to interpret the symbols in your dream and the context in which they appeared in order to understand what your dream is telling you.

The Dream's Context

The context or setting of the dream tells you what it is about. For instance, if the dream takes place in a school, it may be telling you it is about learning something. If it takes place in a hospital or doctor's office, it may be telling you the dream is about health and healing. If it takes place while you are driving in a car, it may be offering you information about the path you are traveling through life. Pay attention to these context clues and interpret them using either your personal symbolism or symbolism from the collective consciousness (see below).

Collective Consciousness Symbols and Personal Symbolism

Next, you need to understand the symbols that appear in your dream and what they mean. Symbols in dreams may come from your own personal symbolism, or they may be symbols from the collective consciousness.

Psychologist Carl Jung theorized something called the collective unconscious, which was basically an energetic grouping of symbols and ideas that exist as part of something called *consensus reality*. As a group, society, or species we subconsciously agree on a certain set of symbols and their general meanings. These symbols for the collective conscious are what you will find in a dream dictionary.

I recommend buying a good dream dictionary (there are plenty available). For a free tool, one of the best online dream dictionaries I've found is at DreamMoods.com. It has a searchable database of thousands of symbols that may appear in your dreams with various interpretations. When using these symbols, keep in mind the various interpretations and listen to your intuition to guide you to the one that seems right for you.

However, before you pick up a dream dictionary and look at symbols from the collective unconscious, consider your own personal symbolism. Ask yourself what you think the dream or symbols mean and see if anything arises. Close your eyes and pay attention. Write down any information you may receive. If nothing arises, then you can turn to symbols from the collective consciousness.

Symbols from the Collective Consciousness

While I can't tell you what your own personal symbols mean, I can offer a basic primer on symbols that are in the collective unconscious. Below is a brief primer on some of the symbols that may appear in your dreams.

Dreaming of Other People

One of the keys in dream interpretation is remembering this: every person you dream of in a symbolic dream is actually an aspect of yourself, so when you dream about another person, you are actually dreaming about yourself. If the person is someone you know, ask yourself which aspects of that person you resonate with in your waking world, or which faults they have you can barely stand. These might give you a clue to the aspect of yourself the dream is talking about. If it is someone you don't know, look for personality traits or features that may be telling you something about yourself.

The other thing another person might represent in your dream is an archetype. Without delving too deeply into Jungian psychology (which is a fascinating topic all of its own), Jung outlined major archetypes that represent aspects of self, desires, fears, etc.

The 12 Major Archetypes

Below are the main archetypes that appear in dreams.

- **Outlaw** - This is your rebellious side. The part of you that fights the power and desires to live outside of the bounds of polite society. The outlaw may represent your desire to change what isn't working in your life or point out areas where you may be causing damage to yourself. Taken too far, the outlaw can become harmful to self and others.
- **Explorer** - This is your desire to get out, experience, learn, and know. Often, the explorer is a call to your soul's true purpose, guiding you to where you need to be to follow your soul's path. On the dark side, the

explorer can avoid creating ties or finding satisfaction in life.

- **Creator** – This represents your creative side! It is your call to action to explore how you create in your own life. The dark side of the creative can be lack of focus or pursuit of vision to the detriment of gaining knowledge and wisdom.
- **Hero** - A call to courage, this is your desire to be the hero in your own story through acts of both everyday courage and extraordinary bravery. At it's darkest, the hero may become the martyr or sacrifice self.
- **Magician** - The magician is the source of alchemy in your life. It invites you to make things happen in your life - and on the dark side, it may be showing you how you are manipulative or feeling manipulated.
- **Sage** - Your wise self, the sage is your call to seek the truth in your life, whatever it may be, through the pursuit of knowledge and understanding. The sage is about more than intelligence, however, it's also about wisdom. At it's darkest, the sage can become a know-it-all with an out of control ego as opposed to one who has gained wisdom through scholarly pursuit.
- **Ruler** - This is the aspect of yourself that is about power and control. On the positive side, power is about personal power and presenting yourself in the world in a powerful way. On the negative side, power can become about ego and control of others.
- **Innocent** – This is often called the Divine Child, because the innocent sometimes comes across in dreams as a beautiful and pure child. The innocent represents your faith and optimism. Taken too far, the innocent archetype can lead to foolishness and blind trust in those who do not deserve it.
- **Regular** - The regular guy/gal is a representation of egalitarianism (equality for all). It is about belonging and lack of pretense. Taken too far, it represents going too far to fit in and losing oneself.

- **Caregiver** - This is about loving and helping others. The caregiver represents selflessness, although taken too far it can represent loss of self or abdication of personal needs to the point of self-exploitation.
- **Lover** - This archetype is about relationship to others - not just romantically, but also via friendship, family, or humanitarian love. It's a recognition of the oneness between all souls. Taken too far, it can become loss of self or desire to please for love and attention.
- **Jester** - The jester represents living in the moment, finding enjoyment in the small things, and living life to its fullest. The jester is lightheartedness, humor, and joy. Taken too far, the jester is frivolity or wasting time.

Common Symbols

While sometimes a cigar is just a cigar (thank you, Dr. Freud), often objects in symbolic dreams mean something other than their literal interpretation.

- **Clothes** in dreams are about how we want to be seen and perceived, or how we are feeling psychologically. For example, if you're wearing a sexy little number, it may suggest you want to be perceived as sensuous, while wearing a huge parka may suggest you wish to stay under cover, or your underwear may suggest you're feeling exposed (and who hasn't had that dream). The context of the clothing is important, as is the color.
- **Vehicles** in dreams are about control in your life. Are you in control of the vehicle, or have the brakes stopped working? Can you steer? Have you lost your vehicle and can't find it? These all tell you something about how in control you are feeling in various aspects of your life. For example, if someone else is driving the vehicle, and you're just a passenger, you may feel that person is controlling some aspect of your life. If you're barreling down hill and can't get the brakes to work,

you may be feeling out of control and in danger of crashing and burning. If you lose your vehicle, you may feel as if you've lost control over some aspect of your life (look to other hints in the dream to tell you what that might be).

- **Dolphins/whales** represent spiritual guidance and inspiration, as well as intuition and awareness. Likewise, dolphins and whales are the living embodiment of the Akashic records on the planet.

- **Water** in dreams represents spirituality, emotions, and the unconscious. With water, look to its state, color, and clarity to provide more context. For example, muddy waters may suggest you are feeling confused or like someone is obfuscating on an issue. Choppy waters (rivers, rough seas) may suggest emotional or spiritual turmoil. Clear waters may represent clarity and clear vision. Calm waters may represent spiritual peace and calm emotions.

- **School** dreams are common anxiety dreams for adults who haven't been in school for years. For example, I have a recurring dream it is finals week at college and I haven't been to class all quarter and haven't a damn clue where my classroom is, much less how I will be able to take the test. This is a very common recurring anxiety dream for people. School in dreams may also represent the desire to learn or the need to gain knowledge/wisdom about something. Look to dream context for other clues.

- **Houses** are about your inner self and who you really are. Different rooms in the house may symbolize different things; for example, the kitchen may be about spiritual or emotional nourishment, while a bedroom may indicate you need to rest.

- **Hospitals** in dreams are about healing. It doesn't necessarily mean physical healing (although sometimes it can). It can also be spiritual, mental, or emotional. If you are in a hospital having surgery, it may suggest it is time to cut something out of your life, or it may be suggesting that you feel you have lost control of your body in some way. Doctors in dreams may also symbolize healing.

- **Killing** in dreams is one of the symbols people find the most disturbing, especially if you are the one doing the killing. However, fear not, if you've never had the waking urge to kill, you probably aren't a closet murderer just waiting to waste someone. Instead, killing in dreams represents your desire to kill a part of your personality either because it doesn't serve you or because it is part of yourself with which you are uncomfortable.
- **Birth** dreams often symbolize creativity because giving birth is creation in its purest form. It can also symbolize new beginnings.
- **Babies** in dreams may symbolize your need to nurture some aspect of yourself, or it may symbolize starting anew.
- **Flying** in dreams can represent spirituality. It can also represent rising above some situation, or it may represent success.

Colors

Color is important in dreams so if a color stands out to you at all (whether it's a color of a shirt, the name of the color, or any other way a color might show up), it's probably meaningful.

- **Light colors** - In general, lighter colors tend to represent positive things, as do very clear colors.
- **Dark colors** - On the other hand, dark colors (colors mixed with a lot of black or very cloudy/muddy colors) may represent negativity.
- **Vivid colors** - The brighter or more vivid a color, the more your subconscious is trying to get you to pay

attention and recall/remember the color and its meaning.

As with all symbols, look to your personal beliefs about the meaning of colors before you look to symbolism from the collective consciousness. Colors may also represent chakra energies. If, however, they don't represent your personal beliefs or the chakras, these are some collective consciousness interpretations.

- **Black** is often representative of the unknown or unconscious. It might also represent your shadow self; that is, an aspect of yourself that makes you uncomfortable. However, it's important to work with your shadows and bring them into the light. Shadow aspects can be used for good in your life because there is duality in everything so you can choose whether it is a positive or negative force.
- **Blue** represents truth, wisdom, and integrity. You can also tie colors in dreams into chakra colors, so blue is the color of the throat chakra.
- **Brown** is the color of being grounded and can represent earthiness, as well.
- **Gold** is the color of spiritual richness and spiritual reward.
- **Green** is the color of healing. It's also a color that represents positive change and growth. It can also represent your heart chakra, which is associated with unconditional love.
- **Indigo** is the color of the Divine. It may also be associated with psychic abilities and spiritual guidance.
- **Orange** is a sociable, friendly color. It's also the color of your second chakra, which is related to your place in family and society.
- **Purple** is more than just the color of royalty. It is also a color of wealth, prosperity, devotion, compassion, and

kindness. It is associated with the sixth (third eye) chakra, as well.

- **Silver** is the color of justice and protection.
- **White** is a color of peace, purity, and new beginnings. It is also representative of the Divine and related to your crown chakra.
- **Red**, which is associated with the root chakra, is a color that may represent vigor, passion, intensity of emotion, shame, or danger.
- **Yellow** is the color of intellect, illness, taking action, and self-confidence. It is also associated with the third (solar plexus) chakra, which is associated with a sense of self.

Numbers

When numbers appear in dreams, they come in various ways. You may actually see, speak, or hear a number. You might also note a certain number of objects, such as two people, four forks, etc. If a number sticks out to you post-dream, it is probably significant.

- 0 - I always think it's funny that 0 is included as a dream symbol number. After all, if there is zero of something in your dream (I had zero pink bunnies in my dream - that must mean 0 was in my dream), is that significant? Of course not, but zero can still appear mostly written, heard, or spoken. If it does stand out to you, it stands for nothingness or empty space. Its presence in a dream might be telling you it is okay to clear space in your life and leave room so other things can enter.
- 1 - This number stands for ego, individuality, or autonomy.
- 2 - If two appears, it speaks of balance, polar energies, yin-yang, or partnership.
- 3 - The number three speaks of inner strength, vitality, and trinities (such as body-mind-spirit, etc.)
- 4 – This is a number of balance and stability. It may also indicate hard work, or things that come in fours, such as

the four directions or four elements (earth, air, water, fire).

- 5 – The number five indicates taking action, boldness, and spontaneity. It may also indicate the five senses.
- 6 – Six represents cooperation, community, union, and bliss.
- 7 - Seven is a number of healing and completion. It may also represent things that come in 7s, such as your chakras or days of the week.
- 8 – This number represents intuition, success, and karma.
- 9 - Nine is a number of inspiration or rebirth. It can also be a number of completion.
- Numbers beyond the first nine are a combination of the meanings of the two numbers (so 63 might indicate inner strength and cooperation. Look to additional context in your dream to give you clues to the meanings of the numbers.

The information I've shared about dreams above is just the tip of the iceberg in dream interpretation

Sample Interpretation

To help you better understand the process in action, I offer a sample interpretation.

I dreamed about playing dodgeball (which later morphed into field hockey and then some weird golf game), and everyone was divided into a yellow or purple team. I didn't get a jersey for either team, and the director of the game kept trying to give me a clear jersey (always great for showing off the bra or greeting your significant other at the door when he comes home from work). I wanted to be on a team; I didn't care which and insisted the director give me a team jersey.

I discovered there was a blonde woman (her name was

Annie) with short hair who had taken my jersey. She was on the yellow team, but she wanted the opportunity to be on either team depending on who was winning or losing. I was upset at this injustice, and I tried to get her to give up my jersey, but she wouldn't.

The director (who had short, dark hair) looked through all the colors and kept giving me colors that weren't either team. I kept insisting on being placed on one of the teams. Finally, she came up with a purple jersey, but it was more violet while the rest of the team was dark purple.

Then I went and joined the game but realized what a slow runner I was. I was adept at playing, but I just wasn't as fast as the other players. Two other teams had joined the game, and nobody was sticking to a team anymore. The teams (the other two colors were blue and red) were all intermingled. So instead, I found a cache of colorful golf balls buried in a hole in the ground and played with that. The cache was at the top of a hill, and I pulled up each colorful ball and tossed it down the hill to a green playing field.

Here are some of the symbols that showed up in my dream:

- A director or overseer
- Blonde woman (Annie) who tried to "steal" my position
- Short hair
- Dark hair
- Blonde hair
- Balls of different types and sizes
- The number two (two teams, two lines)
- Wanting to be part of a team
- Sports

- Teams
- Running
- Various colors with the most predominate colors being purple, yellow, violet, and white/clear
- Jerseys
- Slow
- Hole in the ground hiding a cache of something

These are the symbols I will start to work with when interpreting the dream. From here, the interpretation is part intuition, part personal symbolism, part collective symbolism, and part self-understanding.

Context

I start by looking at the context of the dream, which is a ball game of some type. I desperately wish to participate. This gives me the overall theme of the dream. It tells me what the dream is about. It is being played on a field that is rough and rocky with lots of hills, but there is a bright green, smooth pitch at the bottom of the dirt hills. In this case, the sport changes throughout the dream, so what is probably important is the field on which it is played, as well as the fact that there are balls in the game.

- A **ball** indicates wholeness and playfulness.
- The **field**, which is the main setting of the dream, is kind of dark (overcast with an overall dark feel), and the terrain is variable and often hazardous. Still, there are also beautiful, flat green parts, as well. This indicates a duality of both abundance and freedom (green field), along with my belief in lack (lack of abundance, etc.). Since both are in my dream equally, it shows I'm struggling in my life with optimism and pessimism at the same time, and neither is

particularly winning out right now. The hills represent obstacles and dirt represents frugality. The overall darkness indicates this is all part of my shadow self, and the dream is telling me something about aspects of myself I wish to hide or not acknowledge.

- In the dream, I am throwing balls down dirt hills to greener fields where the balls can come into play again. So I am tossing my wholeness away from pessimism and darkness towards optimism and joy once again. I am tossing it away from the darkness, pessimism, and lack of abundance towards the abundant and optimistic play field.

People in the Dream

Next, I look at other people in the dream, realizing others in dreams are aspects of self.

- Annie was blonde with short hair. She took something that belonged to me, leaving me to feel as if there was an injustice there. Annie is an aspect of me. Blonde is often a symbol of needing to be more carefree and joyful. Annie (or variations such as Anna, Anne, etc.) is a name I often use for characters in short stories, so it represents some subconscious aspect of myself that comes to fore, perhaps an idealized version of myself. That Annie is a female shows some archetypal aspect of the feminine, such as caring, passivity, nurturing, etc.
- The director of the game was also a woman. She had short, dark hair. Short hair is suggestive of downsizing or masculine aspects. Dark hair depicts an aspect of mystery or shadow. The fact the woman is a director shows she is

somehow in charge or a leader. She has control over the duality or the game.

Both of these people are aspects of myself, and they played a big role in the dream and my emotions there.

Looking at the two women who were main characters and the cues provided here, I am seeing them as the yin and yang aspects of myself. One side is fair, open, empowered, a little bit mysterious, and decisive but at the same time isn't arriving at decisions quickly enough for my tastes. The other side is more carefree but also passive and not always as honest or forthright as she can be, probably out of self-protection or a desire to be a certain way (in this case she wanted to be on a winning team and was therefore deceptive in her practices). I see her as behaving unethically and blocking me from something I want.

I was equally frustrated with both women, but for different reasons. This shows me there are aspects of both my yin and my yang that still frustrate me or make me unhappy. However, in the end I prevail with both women and am allowed to enter the playing field, which suggests I am consciously working to accept my shadow self in order to bring it into the light of my consciousness.

Colors and Numbers

Next, I look at other supporting symbols and how they fit within the context of the dream to tell me more about the situation.

- **Numbers:** The number two is a very strong symbol that repeats throughout the dream (two teams, two more teams, two women, two lines, etc.), telling me it is something important. Two suggests balance and yin and yang, which is reinforcing one of the main themes I've already discovered.

- **Colors:** The four main colors of yellow, purple, violet, and clear/white are as follows: Yellow is self-confidence, intellect, and taking action; purple is loyalty, wealth, kindness, intuition, and compassion. Violet is spirituality and intuition. White is peace and new beginnings. These are supporting the main theme of the dream: that I am struggling between two aspects of self—intellect and compassion perhaps—and that I am also trying to overlay it with a sense of peace or Divinity. Ultimately, compassion prevails (I wind up on the purple team), although it is more focused on spirituality and intuition than wealth and compassion.

Other Symbols

The dream has many other symbols, which support the themes I have identified.

- Teams (which are filled with my friends, by the way) are about relationships, friendships, and working together. The fact I am unhappy I am not part of one or the other suggests I am struggling with a relationship in my real life, and I long for resolution.
- Sports indicate recognition of talents and achieving my goals. I want this very badly in my dream, but I realize I'm a slow runner (however, I am adept at the sport. I'm just not quick), which suggests the (self) recognition of talents and achievement of goals is coming more slowly than I would wish.
- The jerseys in the dream are just a way to convey the colors, which they do. The balls are different colors, as well.
- The hole in the dirt suggests hidden aspects of self, but it is filled with a cache of colorful balls, which indicate wholeness and various aspects of my personality. I dig

up the balls and toss them down the hill, tossing each aspect of self from dark to light.

Putting It all Together

Finally, I look at the entire dream and place it in the context of what is going on in my life to arrive at an interpretation.

This dream is about some frustrations I had. It suggests at the time I felt I was somehow falling behind, particularly spiritually and as it relates to prosperity/abundance, relationships, and my feelings about how my life was going.

At the time, I was experiencing some impatience with myself because I was struggling a bit spiritually. It may help to know at the time of the dream, I was recovering from a concussion. The dream occurred about two weeks after the concussion, and I hadn't yet returned to my usual sunny self, which led to frustration about several things in my life including my professional and spiritual growth, my prosperity and abundance, and a few relationships that had been giving me trouble.

Normally when I feel I'm not winning at life, I'm able to go to my happy place and bring about changes through positive thinking, etc. However, when I had the concussion I felt blocked in my ability to do that due to some cognitive changes associated with the head injury.

However, this dream, while it showed me my frustration, also showed me I was moving in the direction of returning to my more customary happy place where I could create and manifest positivity with my thoughts, words, and actions. It showed me I was, through my own thoughts and actions, ultimately returning to that place even though I was frustrated in the moment.

I believe Annie was a manifestation of my frustrations with my concussion, while the director showed me that—while I was a bit confused in the moment—ultimately I would return to the place where I was in charge of my thoughts and actions and how they manifested in my life.

How to Use Your Dreams for Vibrational Healing

The information about interpreting dreams is interesting, but how do you use it as part of your process of vibrational healing? Use the information your dreams provide to help you identify where you need healing. As I've said many times, awareness is an essential first step in healing, followed by intention. Your dreams are a fast track way to recognize imbalances and issues, allowing you to bring your knowledge of them from the subconscious into your conscious mind. From there, you can set your intention to heal and begin to use your other vibrational tools to start rebalancing the energy.

Chapter 9 – Cultivate Joy

Experiencing joy whenever possible is one of the fastest ways to raise your overall vibration, and the experience of joy can help you heal energetic imbalances. This is especially true when you are in circumstances that are less than ideal and feel you're struggling with life. You can do this even in the worst of circumstances, which can instantly raise your vibration and help set healing in action so you can work your way out of whatever difficult circumstance you are experiencing. In fact, it is the darkest times that make the moments of joy seem so bright, because, in life, you can't truly appreciate the sweet without the bitter.

A Personal Experience with Joy

I have had anything but a perfect life. I am twice divorced (three times married). One of my ex-husbands took me to court for nuisance lawsuits several times (he never won). I had a less than idyllic childhood. I lived in poverty for most of my 20s. I've been fired and laid off from jobs during rough economic times. I had health problems for much of my adult life, including a chronic condition resulting from an automobile accident when I was 21 that left me in pain almost every day. I have extreme food allergies that leave me unable to eat anything with gluten or dairy.

My life, on the surface, is far from perfect, but I am perfectly content. In fact, I'd say I'm downright joyful most of the time. That's not to say I don't have bad days or bad moments. Sometimes, things suck beyond all measure, and in the moment I experience that emotional pain, I allow myself to wallow in its grip until I choose to be happy once again.

That's what I am most of the time. I'm happy, and it is a

deliberate choice I make. When it comes to happiness, I am a ride or die kind of chick. In general, it is my natural state of being.

Joy Is a Choice

I understand that to many experiencing dark times, this may sound like pie in the sky promises, but nothing can be further from the truth. Happiness is possible in any circumstance if you simply choose it.

A Formula for Joy

The formula for joy is quite simple. In each moment, choose who you wish to be. There's one true fact in our 3-dimensional, embodied universe: this moment is all we have. We can't do a darn thing about the past, and we have no way of predicting the future. Both are illusions. But this moment, right now, it is the only real thing you have. So why, in this moment, would you choose anything but happiness?

Do you know how I know the past is illusory? Have you ever heard two different people describe the same event? If you have, you've probably noticed a big discrepancy in the varying descriptions of the exact same thing. This discrepancy arises from the fact that as soon as a moment has passed, we immediately begin to process it through our own set of filters, which give us each a unique point of view. Those filters consist of attitudes, past experiences, self-image, and a myriad of other factors that influence how we think and experience the world.

Be in the Moment

In the moment when an event is occurring before we've had a second to process it through our minds and egos, we all experience it in the same way. Immediately after the fact, however, we begin to tell stories about what we saw. We assign motives we can't possibly know to be the truth. We add our own feelings and prejudices. We begin the process of interpretation and justification that allows us to shape what we have just experienced to suit our own world-view and self-image.

In the moment, however, all we have is experience. We have no judgments about what it might mean, nor do we have any concerns about how it may affect our futures. We just have this moment right now, which is pure experience.

Sometimes in the moment, that experience hurts, it's true. But I always believe this: I can experience anything for just one moment. So I allow the hurt until I'm ready for it not to hurt any longer. I find if I give myself the full experience of pain in the moment, it wanes quickly and I am once again ready to cultivate joy.

Finding Joy During Times of Pain

If you're going through something painful, how do you cultivate joy? You do so by giving yourself moments that bring you joy. Engage in an activity about which you are passionate and allow yourself to be there in that moment without letting your thoughts wander to the past or the future. Spend time with someone you love. Laugh. Wrestle with a puppy. Smell a flower. Sit outside with the sunshine on your face. And for those moments, allow yourself to experience joy, in spite of the circumstances.

Someone—I can't for the life of me remember who—once gave me an example of cultivating joy in the moment that I found extremely profound.

"Imagine," he said, "Sitting on the grass in the sunshine. Listen to the birds chirp. Tilt your head back and look at the cloudless blue sky. Allow the sunlight to warm your face, your arms, your hair. It's perfect. It's beautiful. Now, imagine you are in the exact same spot, but this time, imagine you are homeless. If you stay in the moment, it is still beautiful regardless of the circumstances or your story. The sun is still shining. The birds are still singing. The air is still perfumed with the scent of freshly cut grass. Does your larger circumstance of being homeless make that moment—you, sitting on the grass in the sunshine— any less beautiful than if you have a big house to go home to?"

My answer to his question was no, as long as you stay in the moment. Here's an example from my life.

My former husband was...one of my greatest teachers. However, at the time my story about him was that he was a douchebag. He had recently told me he'd slept with someone else while I was away visiting my parents. Suddenly, my life had the very real possibility of becoming an episode of the *Jerry Springer Show*. I was furious, betrayed, hurt, hostile, terrified, and everything in between. My insides felt like they would chew up my entire body until I disappeared completely.

Still, I had a child and had to maintain some type of normalcy for him. So there I was, in the kitchen, fuming, hurting, crying, and everything in between. It was a beautiful spring afternoon, and I had the kitchen window open. A slight breeze was blowing the curtains back and caressing my cheek as I stood at the counter shelling peas. The sunlight slanted in through the window and shone on my hands, which were engaged in the satisfying snapping of opening the pods. The sweet, earthy scent of the peas surrounded me, along with the smells of springtime that arrived on the gentle breeze. As I centered myself in these sensations, everything else faded away. The tears stopped, and peace descended. In that moment, in some of the deepest turmoil I had ever experienced in my life, I felt joy.

This was the moment I discovered the secret of inner joy in spite of outer circumstances. To cultivate joy in the midst of darkness, do this: engage in something you love and be fully present for the experience. Let the past fade away and just be here now. Don't filter. Don't think. Don't justify. Just be. Do this as often as you can, no matter what your circumstances. In doing so, you just may cultivate a happier life.

Engage in Activities that Bring You Joy

The activities in which you engage also have a vibration. Your Divine guidance system tells you which activities are beneficial, and which might lower your vibration. For instance, my Divine guidance system is not a fan of violent television and movies, but it seems to love dancing. That's not to say I never watch television or go to movies, but I tend to spend more time engaging in the activities my Divine guidance system loves (and that I love) and less time doing the things that are less beneficial. I skew towards activities that bring me joy, and in doing so this allows me to bring joy into other, traditionally less joyful activities (like vacuuming).

Listen to your Divine guidance system. It will guide you to joy if you allow it.

Chapter 10 – Create a Sense of Purpose

Everyone wants to feel as if they are living a meaningful life. However, sometimes during times of strife or stress, it can be difficult to discover just what purpose your life truly has. It's natural from time to time to feel like you've lost your sense of forward movement; your feeling of contributing to something greater than yourself. These feelings may arise during times of contentment when you're feeling safe and secure within your overall life situation. They may come when your children grow up and move away. They may come when you're working a job that just doesn't seem to allow you to contribute anything meaningful in the world.

I understand. At several times throughout my life, I've felt adrift and as if my life was lacking in purpose. Most often, these times of what I felt were aimlessness were actually the periods that immediately preceded my finding a new, greater sense of purpose.

How Purpose Affects Vibration

Having a sense of purpose provides a driving force that gives you a roadmap of where you want to be. This sense of purpose allows you to be proactive instead of reactive, because with a sense of purpose you make choices to move you towards that. When you don't have a sense of purpose, you are more likely to feel you are at the mercy of everything around you and react to it. Once you have a sense of purpose, you can set your intentions and from your intentions, you can choose your thoughts, words, and actions. It is through these means that your sense of purpose affects vibration. Without purpose, you may experience energetic blockages, or your thoughts, words, and deeds may be inconsistent and reactive instead of consistent and proactive, causing you to slip out of balance energetically.

What to Do if You Feel You Lack Purpose

What I've discovered in my own life, however, is a sense of purposelessness isn't always a bad thing. It doesn't have to mean you are driving a rudderless ship. Instead, if you feel your life lacks purpose right now, reframe how you think about it. Instead of thinking, *I am without purpose*, think instead, *I am in state of openness where I am ready for something new and significant to enter my life*. You can even use this as a meditation mantra or affirmation.

Reframing purposelessness as readiness is a way of setting intention and typically, it doesn't take much time after you rephrase it before something new enters and you to feel directed and driven as you move forward towards something important.

If you feel your life is currently lacking purpose and meaning, here are some strategies to try to help as you move forward.

1. Acknowledge the Feeling

Simply acknowledging something brings it to light and spurs the process of change. Instead of ignoring it, allow yourself to truly feel your purposelessness, noting how it feels in your body, mind, and spirit. Be with the feeling with no requirements other than the experience that it is there.

2. Reframe It

Once you've been with the feeling for a while, redefine it. Is it purposelessness you are feeling, or are you in a state of open readiness, willing to accept what the universe brings next? Being in a state of open readiness lets the universe know you are ready and willing for something new and significant.

3. Set Your Intention

Intention is the precursor to action. Deliberately (aloud, in writing, in prayer, in meditation, or however you talk to the universe) state your intention for new purpose to come into your life. In other words, ask for it. Express gratitude that before you have asked, the universe has already answered, and it is on the way.

4. Don't Force It

Being without purpose can feel empty, but that doesn't mean you should force yourself into something new just for the sake of having a purpose. Events in the universe take time to unfold sometimes, and it would be a shame to be tied up with busywork and totally miss it when the thing you've been seeking comes along. Likewise, trying to force purpose may limit the universe, which is prepared to bring you the very thing you need if you allow it.

5. Say Yes!

When you exist in a state of open readiness, the universe will bring you exactly what you need, but it's still up to you to say yes when it arrives. How will you recognize it? Because inside, there will be a knowing that, whatever it may be, this is the right thing for you to do, the right path for you to follow, and the exact place you need to be. Don't let fear of the unknown hold you back. When the opportunity arises, grab it with both hands expressing gratitude the universe provided you with exactly what you needed when you needed it.

6. Make Room While You Wait

We all have stuff in our lives—physical things, emotional baggage, old beliefs and habits, busywork, activities we don't really want to do or care about, relationships that no longer serve us or drain us, etc.—that are things we do or have that don't really enrich us in any way. All this junk takes up space in our lives that may keep us from having room for something really fabulous to come in. If we're overloaded with things that don't matter, we feel overwhelmed and as if we lack money, time, space, etc. to allow even one more thing to enter our lives.

So, while you await purpose, make room for it. Clear out junky closets. Step away from relationships that don't serve you. Set boundaries with others and stop saying yes to things you want to say no to. Eliminate activities you no longer enjoy or that no longer serve you. Take inventory of thoughts and beliefs and discard those that don't serve you. The goal here is to make space in your life by clearing out things you don't want, need, or enjoy so you have room for things you do.

Embracing the Space

It's natural from time to time to feel like your life lacks purpose, but these times don't need to be difficult. Instead of feeling lost or empty, know the universe is conspiring in your favor to bring you the perfect opportunity you need to move forward in the interest of your greatest and highest good. In the meantime, move into the space in gratitude, knowing you are sitting in a place of readiness for the perfect opportunity to come along that will support you on your path.

Chapter 11 – Sound

Sound occurs due to vibration. When something sounds, it vibrates in waves through a medium, such as air or water, which causes that medium to vibrate. When we hear a sound, it is because the vibrations hit our eardrums, which also begin to vibrate, and the brain perceives these signals as sound. However, even if you didn't have eardrums, the vibration of sound waves would still enter your body and, through entrainment, cause a vibrational shift.

For example, consider infrasonic sound, which is a very low frequency many humans cannot detect (others can). Studies have shown exposure to infrasound can cause feelings of fear in humans, even if they don't hear it and are therefore unaware the sound is present. The vibration from the sound still has an effect that produces a result in the human body.

Try this. Close your eyes and hum a long tone. As you sustain this hum, notice where you feel it in your body and how it feels. If you're humming a traditional hum sound, "hmmmmmmm," you'll likely feel a tickling in your nose, cheeks, and face. That is the vibration from the sound causing the bones in your face to vibrate as you hum.

The Effects of Sound

Sound is evocative and can contribute to various emotions and feelings. For instance, think about the music that plays in the background of television shows or movies. Without even realizing it, that music helps draw you into the story you are watching by setting an emotional tone with the chords and notes (tones) it uses, its tempos, instrumentation, and the overall feel of the piece.

For example, think about the song *Sound of Silence.* Find two versions of this song on YouTube: The folk duo Simon and Garfunkel's original recording and the 2015 version recorded by the metal band Disturbed. Although the melody and lyrics are the same, chances are you'll step away from one with a different set of emotions and feelings than you'll have when listening to the other. Something in the music provides a different vibration although it's the same song.

However, even the sounding of a single tone or note has a unique vibration. The frequency of the note determines its tone, pitch, and octave. In sound healing, you can use single tones to help entrain energetic systems in order to clear imbalances.

The Frequency of Sound

Different tones or notes have different frequencies. Frequency is a measure of how many cycles (in this case, sound wavelengths) occur in a unit of time. In sound, this is measured as hertz (Hz) or kilohertz (kHz). Sub-audio (or subsonic) tones have a frequency of <20Hz (less than 20 hertz). The frequency at which human ears can perceive sound is between 20Hz and 20 kHz (20,000 hertz), and ultrasonic (high frequency) tones above which a human ear can typically perceive are >20kHz (greater than 20,000 hertz).

Note, Pitch, and Octave

Without geeking out too much on music theory, I think it's important to offer some basic definitions as we move forward so we are on the same page as far as the terms I use.

- **Pitch** is a frequency of sound. So a sound's pitch might be 440Hz, which is the note middle A (also known as A_4). There are far more pitches than notes (see the 12 notes below), because every change in frequency changes the pitch.

- **Note** is a named pitch tuned to a standard frequency. In the example above, 440Hz is the note middle A, sometimes noted as A_4. In music, there are 12 notes. Frequencies listed are all in the same octave as A_4: C (262 Hz), C# (C-sharp, 278Hz), D (294Hz), D# (311Hz), E (330Hz), F (349Hz), F# (370Hz), G (392Hz), G# (415Hz), A (440Hz), A# (466Hz), B (494Hz)
- **Octave** is an interval between two pitches where the frequency doubles. So, 220Hz would be A_3 one octave lower than A_4, while 440Hz would be A_5, one octave higher.

Sounds and the Chakras

Different sounds are associated with different chakras. These can be individual tones, such as musical notes and pitches, or they can be sounds you physically make, such as vowel sounds or mantras. Each of these tools (we'll go into detail in later sections) has its own frequency which acts on your energetic centers and can help cause entrainment to balance vibration. Therefore, if you have a chakra that is out of balance, you can use sound to affect it. Pitches, notes, and frequencies associated with each chakra follow. The octaves of the notes do not matter – all affect the same chakras. Therefore, all are noted below in the middle octave of C_4 through B_4. Frequency ranges are approximate.

Root Chakra
Note: C (262Hz) or C# (278Hz)

Pitches and Frequencies: 256Hz through 285Hz

Sacral Chakra
Note: D (294Hz) or D# (311Hz)

Pitches and Frequencies: 286Hz through 320Hz

Solar Plexus Chakra
Note: E (330Hz)

Pitches and Frequencies: 321Hz through 340Hz

Heart Chakra
Note: F (349Hz) or F# (370Hz)

Pitches and Frequencies: 341Hz through 385Hz

Throat Chakra
Note: G (392Hz) or G# (415Hz)

Pitches and Frequencies: 386Hz through 425Hz

Third Eye Chakra
Note: A (440Hz) or A# (466Hz)

Pitches and Frequencies: 426Hz through 480Hz

Crown Chakra
Note: B (494Hz)

Pitches and Frequencies: 481Hz through 511Hz

All of the tools you will use that are tuned to pitches and frequencies will actually be tuned to a specific standard note. The ranges in the pitches and frequencies noted above account for variability in tuning. I've gotten a little over technical here for the sake of explanation. When working with tools that produce notes, simply look for notes and the frequencies of that specific note or the octaves of the frequencies mentioned above.

Tuning Forks and Singing Bowls

Tuning forks and singing bowls have pure vibrations that resonate at the specific frequency of certain notes. Generally, these instruments are carefully tuned and vibrate at the exact frequency of the tuned note.

Tuning Forks

You can buy a complete set of tuning forks for under $200, and some are quite affordable. Tuning forks vibrate when you strike them. Holding them close to the body and to the area you wish to balance energetically generates entrainment.

Types of Tuning Forks

There are several types of tuning forks.

- Solfeggio tuning forks are tuned to the six solfeggio frequencies (see below). Solfeggio tuning forks are best for working with deep seated emotional and spiritual imbalances.
- Chakra tuning forks are tuned to the frequency for each chakra. These are good for clearing blockages and rebalancing chakra energy.
- Weighted tuning forks, which have round weights on the ends of each fork, are best for working with body issues and correcting energy imbalances resulting from physical blockages. Weighted tuning forks vibrate the longest of any of the tuning forks and produce the strongest and loudest tone. They also don't produce any harmonics or octaves, so they work best for simple physical issues.
- Unweighted tuning forks are best for working with etheric, emotional, and spiritual issues. They don't ring as long as weighted tuning forks, but they produce a wide range of harmonics and octaves within a single tone,

which makes them ideal for complex emotional and spiritual issues.

There are two different methods you can use when working with tuning forks.

- Holding the fork by its handle, tap it on the side of your knee next to your kneecap (but not on it), striking the side of the fork along one prong against your knee. Then, bring the tuning fork up near your ear and listen to the vibration for as long as it lasts. Focus on the vibration and sound. If your mind drifts, gently return your attention to the sound. Do this two or three times.

- Holding the tuning fork by its handle, tap it on the side of your knee next to your kneecap, striking the side of one of the fork prongs against the side of your kneecap. Bring the tuning fork to the chakra with which it corresponds. Hold it an inch or two above your body. Allow it to continue vibrating until it stops. Repeat two or three times. During this, you can close your eyes and visualize the chakra as a glowing ball of colored light spinning in one direction or another.

Singing Bowls

You will find singing bowls tuned to each of the notes on a scale. You may find bowls tuned to different octaves, but remember the note corresponds with the chakra, so octave doesn't matter. Singing bowls tend to be a little more expensive than tuning forks, and the higher the quality of the bowl, the more expensive it may be. Quality and materials affect how long the bowl will ring when played, how deeply it vibrates, its volume, and the purity and pitch. You can buy singing bowls as a set or purchase them one at a time.

Types of Singing Bowls
There are two main types of singing bowls.

- Metal singing bowls are often made of bronze or a combination of metals selected for quality of tone and ability to hold the vibration. Metal singing bowls tend to be less expensive than crystal singing bowls (although some well-made metal singing bowls can be quite expensive). Typically, a set of singing bowls has seven bowls, one for each chakra. They come with wooden mallets for striking and ringing the bowl. You can hold smaller bowls in your hand when you play them.
- Crystal singing bowls are made from a silica quartz. Some may have grains of other crystals infused in the bowls. For example, I have one that is silica and moldavite, a stone formed from a meteorite. Crystal singing bowls tend to be fairly expensive. They have a pure tone that resonates for a long time, and they can be quite loud and impressive. I can feel the vibrations coming from my crystal singing bowls when I play them, something I am less likely to notice with my metal bowls. These bowls come with a rubber or wooden mallet for striking and playing. They also come with a small ring they sit on. The bowls are large, so you need to set them on the ring on a table or the floor. The ring allows them to vibrate freely without interference from the surface they are in contact with.

How to Use Singing Bowls
With small metal singing bowls, extend your non-

dominant hand in front of you with the palm up, and extend your fingers and thumb backwards as far as they will go so the area of your hand just below your fingers forms a ridge. Place the bowl on this ridge. Hold the wooden mallet in your dominant hand. Strike the rim of the bowl percussively with the wooden mallet. You can choose to let this ring, or you can then hold the wooden mallet perpendicular to the rim with one point of the mallet touching one point of the rim and run the mallet around the outside of the rim. This will intensify the ringing.

With the crystal singing bowls, place them on their ring on a solid, flat surface (I typically do this on the floor because tables can move and vibrate). Sit in front of the bowl holding the rubber mallet in your dominant hand. With the tip of the rubber mallet, percussively strike the outside rim of the singing bowl so it starts to ring. You can allow the ring to continue until it dissipates, or you can increase the vibration and ringing after percussively striking it by holding the mallet perpendicular to the singing bowl and running the edge of the rubber ball around the inside or outside edge of the singing bowl's rim.

Getting the bowls to ring by running the mallet along the rim takes some practice. Play with angle, pressure, and speed to get a sound that works for you but always start the sound by percussively striking the bowl first.

You don't need singing bowls to benefit from their vibration. While there's no substitute for the power of the vibration from the live playing of a singing bowl, you can still receive the benefits by listening to recordings. There are plenty available online, and many free versions on YouTube you can use for meditation.

Solfeggio

Using solfeggio requires no special equipment. You can find various tools online and smartphone or tablet apps that offer solfeggio tuning. In fact, YouTube has several. The smartphone app I use for solfeggio is Glenn Harrold's solfeggio for iPhone. It costs a few bucks to download the app, but it's a valuable tool for balancing chakra energy.

Solfeggio frequencies come from an ancient six tone scale commonly used in Gregorian chants. Gregorian chants are believed to have great power that can bring about spiritual harmony. Taking the tones used on this scale, there are six main solfeggio frequencies that roughly correspond to the various chakras.

- 396Hz solfeggio is associated with the color red and the root chakra. It can help you work with guilt and fear.
- 417Hz is associated with the color orange and the sacral chakra. It can help you to make changes in your life.
- 528Hz is associated with the color gold and the solar plexus chakra. It is said to be the solfeggio of DNA repair and can help you work with personal and spiritual transformation.
- 639Hz is associated with the color green and the heart chakra. This is the relationship solfeggio.
- 741Hz is the solfeggio of intuition and can help you awaken psychic energy and connection to your higher self. It is associated with the throat and third eye chakras.
- 852Hz is the solfeggio of spirituality and connection with the Divine. It is associated with the color white and the crown chakra.

You'll notice the frequencies of solfeggio don't quite correspond with the previous information about which frequencies align with the chakras as noted above. The reason actually has to do with the history of the solfeggio. Originally distilled from Benedictine and Gregorian chants and the six note scales, solfeggio arrived at their current state in the 1970s when herbalist Dr. Joseph Puelo had a vision of the frequencies of repeating codes found in *The Bible's* book of *Numbers*. Acting on his vision, Puelo completed a series of complicated mathematical equations based on these repeating codes and, from there, arrived at the six healing tonal frequencies, which are widely used by sound healers throughout the world.

Music

Listening to live or recorded music, playing an instrument, or singing can also help adjust your frequency. Listen to music that is uplifting with harmonic sounds. For raising vibration, avoid dark pieces that are non-harmonic or have jarring sounds. Instead, choose music that makes you feel light, happy, joyful, spiritual, loving, compassionate, or evokes other positive emotions.

You can select music using your Divine guidance system. Ask your guidance system which music can best help you achieve balance and listen for the response. Classical, spiritual, and New Age music are all examples of uplifting sounds.

Masaru Emoto, who did the experiments about how words affected water, did the same with music, exposing water to different types of music before freezing it and photographing the ice crystals. The results were similar to his other experiments. Water exposed to dark music, heavy metal, and similar genres were often dark, muddy, and chaotic while those exposed to spiritual and classical music had ordered and beautiful crystals. You can see the photos at his website at masaru-emoto.net.

Binaural Beats

Binaural beats affect vibration via entrainment by using various sound frequencies to bring about specified changes in brain waves. By themselves, they aren't super pleasant sounding with weird noises and strange pulsing, but when embedded in other sounds, such as music or sounds of nature, the result can be quite uplifting, relaxing, and pleasant. Jim and I use a specific binaural beat every night (under the sound of the ocean) to help deepen our sleep. You can also use binaural beats for meditation, enhanced concentration, lucid dreaming, generating altered states, and many others.

There are dozens of binaural beat apps available for smartphone and tablets, and you can also find them online. I even have an alarm clock that uses nature sounds and binaural beats. They are fun to play with and can help with many aspects of your life.

Vowel Sounds

Toning vowel sounds can cause vibration in different chakras. To use this method, close your eyes and place your hands over the chakra for the vowel sound you are chanting. Take a deep breath and tone the vowel sound for as long as you can. Do it for three to seven times per chakra. For more intense chakra work, do an entire meditation session with a single vowel sound as your mantra. The vowel sounds for the chakras are as follows:

- Root chakra – Uhhhhhh (as in bun or sun)
- Sacral chakra – Ooooooo (as in you or do)
- Solar plexus – Ohhhhhh (as in row or snow)
- Heart chakra – Eye (as in sigh or cry)
- Third eye chakra – Ayyy (as in day or play)
- Crown chakra – Eeee (as in bee or see)

Bija Mantras

Each chakra has its own single syllable mantra. These are known as the Bija mantras. To use the mantras, take a deep breath and then speak the syllable, drawing it out. For focus on a single chakra, close your eyes and place your hands over that chakra. Visualize the chakra as a glowing, spinning ball of colored light as you repeat the mantra over and over, for as long as you like. You can also chant the mantras one after another, working your way up the chakras and visualizing each as you chant the corresponding mantra. The mantras for each chakra are as follows:

- Root chakra–Lam (pronounced laaaaaam with an a sound as if you are saying ah)
- Sacral chakra–Vam (pronounced fvaaaaaaam with a short a, like at)
- Solar plexus chakra–Ram (pronounced with a slight roll of the R and the am pronounced as ahm – so rrahm)
- Heart chakra–Yam (pronounced yum – like you're saying something is delicious)
- Throat chakra-Ham (pronounced hum – like you're humming)
- Third eye chakra–Om (pronounced aummmmmm or ohmmmmm)
- Crown chakra–None – silence

If you have difficulty with pronunciation, you can find many yogis on YouTube chanting the mantras. However, remember intention is key here, so while you would like to honor the sound, you don't need to get too caught up in the technical details.

Pineal Toning

Pineal toning helps awaken your pineal gland, which is

in the center of your brain. Your pineal gland is your connection to the Divine, so awakening and stimulating it with pineal toning can help strengthen your ability to communicate with your higher self and help to tune you in to your Divine guidance system.

Dr. Todd Ovokaitys developed pineal toning as a way to become centered. He believes the tones can help with health and spiritual balance. To learn more and hear examples, visit Dr. Todd's website at pinealtones.com.

To use pineal toning:

1. Sit comfortably with your eyes closed breathing deeply.
2. Visualize your pineal gland as a glowing ball of white light in the middle of your brain. Watch the pulsations of the light as you visualize and listen for the frequency it emits.
3. As you focus on your glowing pineal gland and its sound, take a deep breath, open your mouth, and tone the sound your pineal gland is guiding you to make. You will know it is the correct tone because it will ring almost like a singing bowl.
4. Continue for as long as you like.

Other Sounds

Other sounds can help you achieve energetic balance, as well. Any sound that serves as a focus point and helps bring you into a place of calm and peacefulness will work. This may be anything, such as:

- Aethos sound meditation from Tom Kenyon and the Hathors
- Rain

- Ocean waves
- Birds singing
- Frogs (one of my favorites)
- The sounds of the jungle or tropics
- Wind chimes
- A heartbeat
- Thunderstorms
- Running water
- Whale songs

When presented with the opportunity to hear sounds that are meaningful to you, turn it into a meditative practice. Sit near the source of the sound, close your eyes, and breathe deeply. Focus on the sound, following it without judgment. As thoughts arise, gently return your focus to the sound. Do this for as long as you like.

Listen for Your Spiritual Frequency

Finally, your own spiritual frequency can serve as a sound that helps you find energetic balance. We all have a spiritual frequency sound we can hear if we listen for it. To find yours:

1. Sit or lie comfortably with your eyes closed, breathing deeply in a quiet room.
2. Tune in to the sounds you hear from your own body. Then, focus on your head. Can you hear a high pitched sound similar to the noise something electronic makes, like a ringing or high pitched squeal? This is your spiritual frequency sound.
3. Listen to the sound, focusing solely on it. Pay attention to anything that arises, such as images, thoughts, or ideas. Don't attach or hold on to them. Simply notice them and let them

drift away, returning to the frequency again. Do this for as long as you like.

If you do this often enough, you may notice the frequency of the sound changes as you do vibrational work. This is a sign your own vibration is rising based on the work you have been doing.

Chapter 12 – Crystals

Crystals are a huge subject that make entire books on their own, so it's difficult to distill everything I want to tell you about them and how they can help vibrational healing in a single chapter, but I'm going to try. They are one of my favorite go-to vibrational healing tools, both because they are beautiful and because they have such a powerful effect on your energetic systems. They are small and portable, make great decorations in your home, and are wearable so you can take a vibrational healing tool with you wherever you go.

Magic Rocks

Crystals are minerals. They're rocks, something many people feel are inconsequential and without their own vibration. This couldn't be further from the truth. Crystals are formed in the Earth over millions of years. They contain the energy of Gaia (the planet Earth, which is a living and conscious being) and of the universe (another living and conscious being), and each resonates at its own frequency. Because of their geometric structure, they hold and store energy. They are living beings with their own consciousness and energetic vibration; however, because they have density, we perceive them as being solid and unmoving. Crystals are a gift to humanity, offering a seemingly solid object with which we can work in order to raise our own vibration. When you work with crystals, they give up their gifts to you. Their energy resonates with yours, and your vibration changes through entrainment.

Working with Crystals

One of the simplest ways of working with crystals is wearing them as jewelry. Many artisans make and sell crystal jewelry, such as necklaces, bracelets, earrings, and rings made from precious and semiprecious gemstones that have vibrational qualities. You can also carry crystals with you in a pocket, keep them where you work, or spread them around your home. You can hold them when you meditate, meditate within a circle of crystals, or place them on your body near the chakras you'd like them to entrain. You can create grids of crystals and either meditate within the grid or use the grid as a focus for your meditations. You can also use crystal grids to direct energy by placing them in locations around your home where the energy is most needed.

Finding Crystals

You can find crystals at dedicated crystal shops, metaphysical stores, and gem fairs. Bead shops sell crystals, as do some craft stores. I've even found them at Home Goods. You can also find crystals online on sites dedicated to selling them, such as HealingCrystals.com, as well as on artisan sites like Etsy, auction sites like eBay, and huge retailers like Amazon.com.

When it's possible, I recommend choosing crystals in person instead of ordering them online. That's because there's an energetic element to crystals. I like to hold them and see if they resonate for me. I do this by holding them in my hand, closing my eyes, and tuning in to the sensations I have. The "right" crystal clicks into place for me, and I can feel it is the one meant for me.

When you go to rock shops (as I like to call them), touch and hold the crystals to see how they make you feel. Listen to your Divine guidance system. Notice changes in how they feel in the palm of your hand: do they feel comfortable or uncomfortable? Do they tingle or vibrate? How do they make your head feel? How do they make your spirit feel? Evaluate how you feel when you're holding that crystal as you make a decision whether to choose it.

Bringing Crystals Home

That's not to say you should never order crystals online. If you do buy a crystal sight unseen and its vibration feels off to you, you can cleanse and charge the crystal (something you should do whenever you bring any new crystal home regardless of where you find it) to remove any energy it has absorbed from other people and locations.

Cleansing Your Crystals

As soon as you bring your crystals home, cleanse them. You should also cleanse your crystals every few weeks to a month (more frequently for those that get heavy use) to clear away any energy they've absorbed so they can continue to vibrate at an optimal frequency. There are multiple methods you can use for cleansing crystals.

- Some people recommend soaking crystals in salt water to cleanse them, but I don't, because salt water may erode some specimens. In order to avoid having this happen, I suggest not using this method at all.
- Place them in a container with a cleansing crystal. The crystal selenite (gypsum) is a cleansing crystal that will cleanse all other crystals, so you can place crystals in a sealed box or bag overnight with the selenite to cleanse it.
- If you have a bed of clear quartz (a geode), you can place smaller crystals on the clear quartz overnight to cleanse it.
- Place crystals in the moonlight overnight to cleanse. You can set them outside or on a

window sill where moonlight streams in. If you cleanse your crystals every time there is a full moon, it's a good way to establish the habit and ensure your crystals are regularly cleansed.

- If you practice any form of hands-on energy healing, such as Reiki or Quantum Touch, you can cleanse your crystals by holding them in your hands and channeling energy to them. This is typically the way I cleanse my crystals.

7 Basic Crystals Everyone Needs

Gaia is abundant in her variety, so there are a lot of different crystals, all with amazing healing properties. You can visit crystal shops regularly for years and still not have every single variety. When faced with the sheer volume of crystals, it can be difficult to know which to choose. This list offers a crystal starter kit that contains seven functional, all-purpose crystals.

1. Clear Quartz

Clear quartz is one of the most useful crystals available. It is versatile. With its clear color, it is a high vibration stone that corresponds with your crown chakra but has many other useful metaphysical properties, as well. Some of the properties of clear quartz follow.

- It amplifies the energy of any other stone you use it with.
- It cleanses other stones.
- It facilitates spiritual growth.
- It helps raise your overall vibration.
- It can activate and balance all of your chakras.

If you are having an issue and don't know what other stone to try, use clear quartz. It will always help and can rebalance energy, regardless of the cause.

2. Citrine

Citrine is a clear yellow stone. Traditionally associated with the solar plexus chakra, citrine has a number of other healing properties, as well. It is a stone associated with abundance and prosperity, so keeping citrine in your cash drawer (if you own a business) or wallet can help stimulate abundance. If you place citrine in the back left corner of your home (from the front door facing inward), it can also stimulate abundance. Citrine also has the following properties.

- It boosts feelings of self-esteem and self-worth.
- It raises your vibration and moves you towards enlightenment.
- It changes negative energy to positive.
- It transforms negative thoughts and beliefs to positive ones.
- It promotes success in your endeavors.
- It cleanses the environment of unwanted energy.
- It never needs to be cleansed or recharged like other stones.

3. Rose Quartz

This beautiful, pink stone is associated with unconditional and romantic love. It is most frequently associated with the heart chakra, and it can certainly help to balance this chakra, but it has other qualities, as well.

- It stimulates compassion and kindness.
- It releases negative emotions arising from betrayal, grief, or hurt feelings.
- It clears anger and resentment.
- It guards against jealousy and envy.
- It balances your higher chakras with your lower chakras.
- It opens your heart.

4. Black Tourmaline

Black tourmaline is a stone associated with the root chakra. It grounds and centers you, and it also protects you from negative energy by absorbing it. Other properties of black tourmaline follow.

- It cleanses dark or dense energy and makes it lighter. This could be from another person, a situation, or even planetary events.
- It is calming for people who tend to be scattered.
- It heals frequent worry or negativity.
- It strengthens your immune system.
- It grounds you.

I carry black tourmaline with me all the time because it helps me stay in my positive and happy bubble as it absorbs the negativity of others. Because black tourmaline is a stone that absorbs so much negative energy, it is imperative you cleanse it regularly. During times of especially dark energy (such as when you're going through stress), cleanse it daily. If the black tourmaline stone breaks, it has absorbed as much negative energy as it can, and you need to discard it and get another piece.

5. Smoky Quartz

Smoky quartz is a stone of positive energy. It lifts your mood and helps you step away from negative thoughts. Other properties follow.

- It transmutes negative energy in a place to positive energy. For example, if you are in a place where some major negative event has occurred (perhaps a fight with a spouse or something else), placing smoky quartz there can help to erase that negativity and turn it into a positive. I actually have smoky quartz sprinkled all around the perimeter of my home and property to turn all energy that moves across it coming towards my house into positive energy.

- It enhances courage.
- It promotes inner strength.
- It is grounding.
- It promotes creativity.

6. Amethyst

My mother-in-law, Glennis, loved anything purple, including amethyst. As a result, I frequently bought her amethyst anything, and it made her happy. I share her love of the color purple. It is a high vibration color associated with your two Divinity chakras, the third eye chakra and the crown chakra. Amethyst can help you connect with your Divine guidance system through psychic insight. It also has numerous other properties, some of which follow.

- It assists with sleep issues, particularly insomnia.
- It aids with dreaming and helping you to remember dreams.
- It blocks nightmares.
- It soothes impatience.
- It is calming.
- It enhances intuition.
- It promotes psychic insight.
- It is a traveler's stone and provides protection during travels.

7. Carnelian

Carnelian is a second chakra stone. It promotes clarity and spurs action, among many other characteristics, including the following.

- It stimulates sexual energy.

- It eases hormonal symptoms, including those arising from menstruation or menopause.
- It improves blood flow.
- It increases life force energy.
- It aids in motivation and moving towards goals.
- It helps you manifest your life's path.

Properties of Crystals

Different crystals have differing properties, which can fill pages and pages (I'm actually starting my second book about crystals as soon as I'm done with this one, so it truly is a subject that can fill volumes). Therefore, I'm going to offer a very basic primer of crystal properties.

Opaque versus Clear

In general, clear crystals amplify while opaque crystals absorb. Therefore, when working with crystals if the issue is one of blockage (for example, physically a blockage might be a kidney stone while a mental, emotional, or spiritual blockage might be feeling stuck in a rut) or low energy, use a clear crystal because it will amplify the energy. If you are working with an issue of too much of something (for example, too much aggression) or with a physical issue that involves too much flow (like high blood pressure), use an opaque crystal that absorbs the energy instead.

Colors

While each crystal has its own special properties, when working with chakra energies in general, the color of a crystal tells you which chakras it resonates with and therefore which chakra issues where it might work best for restoring balance.

Root Chakra

The following crystals are beneficial for the root chakra. In general, root chakra crystals tend to be black, gray, or red.

- Hematite
- Black tourmaline
- Obsidian
- Jet
- Red or black sardonyx
- Ruby
- Apache tears
- Black agate
- Black spinel
- Boji Stones® or Kansas Pop Rocks
- Bloodstone
- Black kyanite
- Smoky quartz
- Cinnabar
- Snowflake obsidian
- Dalmatian jasper
- Flint
- Magnetite
- Red jasper
- Red aventurine

Sacral Chakra

Crystals for the second chakra tend to be orange or brown in color, and include the following (among many others).

- Carnelian
- Orange kyanite
- Orange spessartite (a type of garnet)
- Sunstone
- Padparadscha sapphire
- Orange calcite
- Amber
- Bronzite
- Iron pyrite
- Peach moonstone
- Fire agate

- Fire opal

Solar Plexus Chakra

Crystals for the solar plexus are typically gold, brown, or yellow. They include the following, among many others.

- Citrine
- Yellow tigers eye
- Iron pyrite
- Gold
- Amber
- Sphene
- Gold tektite
- Epidote
- Golden obsidian
- Golden healer stone
- Yellow topaz
- Lemon quartz
- Yellow jasper
- Yellow tourmaline
- Yellow kyanite

Heart Chakra Stones

In general, heart chakra stones are green or pink. There are many, a few of which are listed below.

- Malachite
- Green aventurine
- Green fluorite
- Green kyanite
- Emerald
- Peridot
- Chyrsoprase
- Moss agate
- Rose quartz
- Rhodonite
- Green jade

- Green apophyllite
- Amazonite
- Danburite
- Unakite
- Fuchsite
- Zoisite
- Pink tourmaline
- Watermelon tourmaline
- Kunzite
- Rhodochrosite
- Moldavite

Throat Chakra Stones

Stones for the throat chakra come in blues of various colors and include the following:

- Sapphire
- Blue kyanite
- Angelite
- Celestite
- Amazonite
- Turquoise
- Aquamarine
- Labradorite
- Lapis lazuli
- Larimar
- Sodalite
- Azurite
- Tanzanite
- Iolite
- Blue calcite
- Blue lace agate
- Blue spinel

Third Eye Chakra

Stones for the third eye chakra are indigo or violet and include the following among many others.

- Amethyst
- Sugilite
- Labradorite
- Indigo kyanite
- Charoite
- Angelite
- Celestite
- Blue chalcedony
- Rainbow fluorite
- Purple fluorite
- Danburite
- Iolite
- Muscovite
- Lavender quartz
- Tanzanite
- Blue zircon

Crown Chakra Stones

Stones for the crown chakra are characterized by their high vibration, so they can be any color as long as they are of a particular vibrational clarity. However, clear stones also tend to be crown chakra stones. Crystals for the crown chakra include the following:

- Apophyllite
- Moldavite
- Clear quartz
- Phenacite
- Danburite
- Brookite
- Herderite
- Petalite
- Azezulite
- Tanzanite
- Scolecite
- Natrolite

- Tibetan tektite
- Herkimer diamond
- Diamond
- Moonstone
- Amethyst
- Angelite
- Celestite
- Azurite
- Selenite
- Opal
- Howlite

My 7 Favorite Crystals

Earlier, I shared the five crystals I feel everyone should have. Now, if it's super cool crystals you're looking for, here are my current seven favorites.

1. Phenacite

The first time Jim and I went to my favorite rock shop near Portland, OR called Mystery Gallery (if you are nearby – check it out!), Jim said to the owner, "She's looking for something she doesn't have. I doubt there's anything she doesn't have."

The owner proved him wrong. He whipped out a tray of phenacite, and I immediately felt all my energy rush to my head. I felt really lightheaded in the giddiest and most fantastic way possible.

Phenacite is a high vibration stone and when you hold it, it moves your energy right up your chakras and into other realms. It's not for the faint of heart, but I absolutely adore mine.

2. Moldavite

Moldavite was formed from a meteorite impact, and that makes it really cool in my book. It's also a high vibration stone. Along with phenacite, it is one of the 12 synergy stones that work together to help raise your vibration.

3. Super 7 (Melody's Stones)

Super 7 is another high vibration stone that is the natural formation of seven different crystals including amethyst, clear quartz, smoky quartz, lepidocrocite, goethite, rutile, and smoky quartz. With so many different crystals in it, they work synergistically and the stone contains the vibration and properties of all.

Super 7 also has numerological alchemy. Inherent in the name and the contents of seven different stones is a sacred number: 7. In numerology, seven is the number of spiritual awakening and growing awareness. It is a number of completion. You have seven chakras. There are seven days in the week, and the earth has seven continents. There are seven colors in a rainbow and seven notes in major and minor musical scales. Many people consider seven a lucky number.

4. Amber

Natural Baltic amber isn't actually a stone. It's petrified sap. Sometimes it has cool prehistoric bugs or plant matter in it. Amber has natural anti-inflammatory properties, and it is lightweight and always feels warm to the touch. It's often used in teething necklaces for babies: the babies wear them; they don't chew on them. The amber helps calm the pain and inflammation associated with teething and other conditions. Try wearing amber near something on your body that's inflamed, it could help.

5. Labradorite

I love labradorite because it's really beautiful, and I resonate with it. I've never come across a labradorite specimen I didn't immediately want to take home. Like opals and moonstone, labradorite has an iridescent quality called diffraction.

Labradorite is also a multi-purpose stone. Because of its colors and iridescence, it is a stone that works with your throat, third eye, and crown chakra.

6. Boji Stones® (Kansas Pop Rocks)

I typically am not a fan of trademarked and branded stones because they can be expensive. Fortunately, you can find a generic version of Boji Stones called Kansas pop rocks which have exactly the same energy and properties.

Kansas pop rocks come in pairs – one is smooth (female) and one is rough (male). The two pairs bring balance, so you always work with them together. Kansas pop rocks are one of the most grounding stones I've ever found. I hold one in each hand, and I can feel my energy sinking deeply into the earth. As one who is not very grounded, I find these stones quite helpful. Boji stones are also stones that help balance aspects of your energy and duality. For instance, they integrate and balance male and female energies or yin and yang.

7. Ametrine

Ametrine is a combination of citrine and amethyst in a single stone. It is exceptionally beautiful with clear purple and yellow colors in it. Ametrine carries the properties of both amethyst and citrine, so it works with the third through seventh chakras, helping to balance energy flowing between all chakras in this range. Each of the stones magnifies the properties of the other, so its more powerful than using either citrine or amethyst alone. It's also a balancing stone that helps balance opposing energies.

Attraction to Stones

You may find (as I have) that at various times you have greater attraction to one stone or another. This is your Divine guidance system talking to you. Always listen and see which stones choose you. When a stone calls to you, there is something in its energy that will be beneficial to this specific point on your path. You may use that stone for a while, and then you may no longer need it. Of course, you can keep the stone because you never know when you'll need it again, but don't attach to any single crystal.

When I was first working with crystals, I had a small pouch of about eight crystals I took everywhere with me. One day I set them down in my bedroom on my dresser. I turned around for a second to pet a dog, turned back around, and the pouch was gone. I searched everywhere for those crystals. I tore apart dresser drawers, went through all my pockets, and dug through the laundry room. They were nowhere to be found. After a while, I forgot about them and found new crystals.

About six years later the crystals started turning up one by one in various places in my home. I had attached to them in my early work with crystals, and the universe was making sure I moved on from them to new energies I needed. When I realized the lesson about attachment, the crystals started returning to me one at a time.

Occasionally, I also find crystals in weird places. These aren't crystals I have purchased, and when I find them they are never a stone I recognize. However, I believe these crystals (which have turned up outside of a hotel room door in an empty hotel [aquamarine] or on my fireplace mantel [golden healer quartz], for example) have come to me because they are energies I need to work with. I believe this because the crystals I received embodied properties of an energy I was working with when they arrived.

Pay attention to your Divine guidance system and allow yourself to work with crystals that call to you. These are the energies you need the most in your life in this moment. Then, allow yourself to hear Divine guidance when it is time to find a new energy to work with.

Chapter 13 - Aromatherapy and Herbs

In vibrational healing, we tend to focus on the senses of touch, sight, and sound because they have obvious vibrational qualities, and we fail to consider other sensory input as vibratory, as well. However, the senses of taste and smell also have a vibrational quality to them. Everything vibrates. All life and matter arises from the energy of vibration. The solidity of what we experience as matter is merely our perception of the density of those vibrating strands that underlie everything.

The Vibration of Life

Essential oils and herbs are imbued with the vibration of life. They come from living beings (mostly plants) that offer themselves as a gift to the souls inhabiting the human body on this planet. Through the use of these Divine tools of vibration, we can bring about balance.

Aromatherapy

Aromatherapy, or the use of scents, is a fairly mainstream practice. People use essential oils to help bring about physical, mental, emotional, and spiritual healing. People have used essential oils for the purpose of healing for hundreds of years.

Choosing Oils

You'll find many lines of essential oils available, such as Young Living, doTerra, Rocky Mountain Oils, Eden's Garden, and many others. I don't recommend any specific brands, although I do have a few favorites based on purity, quality, and price. When selecting essential oils, try to find those that are made from organic sources with a high standard for quality control. Any of the brands I listed above do this. Likewise, be sure you are using essential oils and not fragrance oils, which are made with synthetic compounds instead of plant essences.

Cautions

I use aromatherapy in my daily life, and I believe it enhances my health and wellbeing. However, there are some cautions it is important to observe in order to use essential oils safely.

- Never apply aromatherapy oils directly to the skin. Instead, dilute them in carrier oils, such as jojoba oil or sweet almond oil. In general, a safe dilution ratio is one drop of essential oil per teaspoon of carrier oil or five to six drops per ounce. This is a dilution of about 2 percent. Failing to adequately dilute essential oils can cause sensitization reactions that can be severe and may include rashes and other uncomfortable or dangerous symptoms.
- Don't consume essential oils unless directed to do so by a professional. Then, use only the oils and dosages they recommend.
- Keep essential oils away from mucous membranes, including eyes, ears, and the nasal lining.
- Some essential oils can cause photosensitivity. Be careful when going in the sun after using them.
- Keep essential oils out of reach of pets and children.
- If you are pregnant or nursing, use essential oils with care and under the supervision of a qualified professional. Some essential oils may cause uterine contractions or be harmful to a baby or fetus. Always research essential oil use and talk with your doctor when you are pregnant and nursing.

- Use caution in using essential oils with babies or very young children. Seek appropriate professional guidance.
- Don't use essential oils made from substances to which you are allergic. For example, if you are allergic to ragweed, you may need to avoid chamomile oil.

Using Essential Oils

There are various methods you can use with essential oils. Some of the most popular are listed below. My favorite methods have an asterisk by them.

- Use diluted in a carrier oil as a massage oil.
- Use in lotions or soaps.
- Put essential oils in a steam cleaner to clean your house.*
- Use them in the laundry. Put a few drops on a sock or wool dryer ball and toss it in the dryer with clothes.
- Diffuse essential oils in a diffuser.*
- Diffuse during meditation.*
- Put a drop of essential oil on a lightbulb.
- Dilute essential oils with water and either witch hazel or alcohol and use as a room or linen spray.*
- Put a few drops in a hot bath.*

Essential Oils for Chakra Healing

Like the other energy healing modalities, certain essential oils resonate more with certain chakras and can help bring about balance if you use them.

Root Chakra
- Cinnamon
- Cedarwood
- Frankincense

- Patchouli
- Benzoin
- Sandalwood
- Ylang ylang
- Vetiver

Sacral Chakra
- Sweet orange
- Neroli
- Carrot seed
- Bergamot
- Clary sage
- Cardamom
- Rosemary

Solar Plexus Chakra
- Lemon
- Grapefruit
- Lemon balm
- Lemongrass
- Lemon verbena
- Chamomile
- Myrrh
- Ginger
- Coriander
- Geranium
- Peppermint

Heart Chakra
- Pine
- Rosemary
- Rose
- Lavender
- Jasmine
- Melissa
- Ylang ylang
- Tangerine
- Yarrow

- Sweet marjoram

Throat Chakra

- Peppermint
- Wintergreen
- Basil
- Spearmint
- Cypress
- Fennel
- Rosewood
- Petitgrain

Third Eye Chakra

- Lavender
- Sandalwood
- Frankincense
- Bay laurel
- Juniper
- Sweet marjoram
- Palo santo
- Nutmeg

Crown Chakra

- Jasmine
- Sandalwood
- Lavender
- Spikenard
- Helichrysum
- Rose

A Few of My Favorite Blends

I like to make my own blends, and I like some premade blends, as well. Below are a few of my favorite.

doTerra Console

doTerra markets this blend as being for grief, but I find it causes my energy to rise up into my higher chakras. It is the essential oil equivalent of phenacite (the crystal), and it's one I use quite frequently because I love how it smells and how it makes me feel.

Edens Garden Meditation

This is a blend I find helps me quiet my mind and focus during meditation. Plus, it smells really good.

Prosperity Blend

This blend helps to remove the blocks to abundance. To make it, combine the following and use it in a diffuser or bath. If you use it in a diffuser, you can eliminate the carrier oil and mix it with water instead:

- 1 ounce of sweet almond oil (carrier oil)
- 3 drops of clove
- 3 drops of sandalwood
- 2 drops of cumin
- 2 drops of cinnamon

Protection Spray

This spray can help keep negative energy away. To make it, mix the following in a spray bottle:

- 4 ounces of purified water
- 1 tablespoon Himalayan pink salt
- 2 drops star anise
- 2 drops of clary sage
- 2 drops of clove
- 2 drops of cumin
- 2 drops of fennel
- 2 drops of ginger

Energy Cleansing and Purification Spray

This spray can transmute negative energy to positive and can consecrate or purify a space for the purposes of meditation or prayer. To make it, combine in a spray bottle:

- 4 ounces of purified water
- 1 tablespoon Himalayan pink salt
- 2 drops of star anise
- 2 drops of basil
- 2 drops of bay
- 2 drops of cedarwood
- 2 drops of eucalyptus
- 2 drops of frankincense

Love Spray

This spray helps bring the energy of unconditional love, compassion, and forgiveness. It is not a love potion, but it can help balance energies to create a space for love. In a spray bottle combine:

- 4 ounces purified water
- 1 tablespoon Himalayan pink salt
- 1 drop of sandalwood
- 1 drop of jasmine
- 1 drop of lavender
- 1 drop of orange
- 2 drops vanilla
- 2 drops cinnamon
- 2 drops clove
- 2 drops ginger
- 2 drops cumin

Migraine or Headache Temple Oil

I used to suffer frequent migraines, so I came up with this formulation, which I would rub on my temples. It helped. In a roll on bottle, mix the following.

- 1 ounce sweet almond oil
- 2 drops of peppermint
- 2 drops of eucalyptus
- 1 drop of rosemary
- 4 drops of lavender

- 1 drop of roman chamomile
- 1 drop of jasmine
- 1 drop of bay

Anti-Anxiety Oil

Calm your anxiety by mixing the following and using it as a temple rub or a massage oil.

- 1 ounce sweet almond oil
- 2 drops of sandalwood
- 4 drops of lavender
- 2 drops of cedar
- 2 drops of clove

Properties of Specific Oils

Below are several essential oils with their specific properties. Observe all safety precautions when using these oils. Based on the properties each contains, you can come up with your own blends.

Bay
- Promotes prophetic dreams
- Aids in purification/cleansing
- Promotes psychic ability

Basil
- Aura cleansing
- Attracts spirit beings
- Protects families
- Removes negativity
- Brings good luck and happiness to new home
- Aids in love relationships
- Assists with forgiveness

Bergamot
- Assists in finding your higher purpose
- Activates Divine guidance
- Purifies

- Promotes inner strength
- Promotes self-confidence

Black Pepper
- Helps you confront fears
- Banishes malevolence
- Spurs action from righteous anger
- Protection against spells
- Dispels evil

Cajeput
- Helps break habits
- Promotes clarity
- Assists with cleansing and purification

Chamomile
- Promotes grounding
- Fosters compassion
- Brings about inner peace
- Releases fear/worry

Cinnamon
- Grounds
- Releases fear
- Improves focus and concentration
- Aids in spirit communication
- Activates Divine guidance system
- Clears energy blockages
- Promotes prosperity

Clary Sage
- Balances chakras
- Connects you with your Divine guidance system
- Helps you understand issues from a spiritual perspective

Clove
- Stimulates kundalini energy
- Provides psychic protection and healing

Coriander

- Stimulates compassion
- Aids in astral projection and OBE experiences

Cumin

- Grounding
- Promotes luck
- Promotes prosperity

Cypress

- Helps you understand the big picture from a spiritual standpoint
- Aids in overcoming loss
- Allows you to let go of pain
- Consecration and protection
- Healing
- Aids in transitions
- Brings blessings
- Eases pain of loss
- Provides comfort and solace
- Promotes inner strength
- Helps you see the immortality of your soul
- Purifies and raises energy
- Removes psychic blocks
- Promotes happiness, peace, harmony, peace, inspiration, and wisdom

Cedarwood

- Purifies
- Promotes physical and spiritual healing
- Eliminates blockages
- Detoxifies (physical, mental, emotional)
- Removes negativity
- Breaks you out of ruts
- Helps you overcome bad habits
- Promotes clarity
- Connects you to spiritual awareness
- Enhances psychic ability

- Promotes harmony, balance, and stability
- Enhances luck and good fortune
- Helps with nightmares
- Associated with happiness and prosperity

Elemi
- Assists with rites of passage
- Facilitates journey to spirit realms

Eucalyptus
- Eliminates and protects against negative energy

Fennel
- Promotes strength and courage
- Protects against negativity
- Purifies
- Facilitates setting personal boundaries and inspiring trust
- Excellent oil for focus during meditation

Frankincense
- Provides protection
- Purifies
- Promotes spiritual love and growth
- Heightens awareness
- Expands consciousness
- Facilitates focus during meditation
- Opens the crown chakra
- Connects you to your Divine guidance system
- Cleansing (body, aura, psychic)
- Removes negativity
- Promotes inner peace and love
- Stimulates prana/qi/life force energy

Geranium
- Protects against negativity
- Balances opposite energies
- Uplifts
- Opens psychic connection

- Facilitates communication

Ginger
- Stimulates self-awareness
- Protects against negativity

Hyssop
- Cleanses the aura
- Consecrates spaces
- Dispels negative energy

Jasmine
- Promotes love and passion
- Stimulates prophetic dreams
- Promotes luck and wealth
- Facilitates balance and harmony
- Promotes justice
- Helps with meditation focus

Juniper
- Transforms negativity
- Provides physical protection
- Purifies
- Helps clear away issues from the past
- Increases psychic abilities
- Strengthens energy field
- Promotes prosperity

Lavender
- Promotes tranquility, harmony, happiness, and joy
- Supports good health
- Helps you sleep better
- Offers psychic protection
- Balances body/mind/spirit, balances yin/yang
- Increases psychic abilities

Lemon
- Uplifts
- Purifies
- Refreshes

- Breaks inertia
- Stimulates compassion

Lemongrass
- Helps remove apathetic attitudes
- Energizes

Lime
- Purifies
- Promotes clarity
- Helps you take action

Mandarin
- Stimulates compassion
- Release negativity – particularly emotional
- Improves self-confidence/self-love

Marjoram
- Promotes compassion
- Grounds
- Helps you overcome fear
- Assists with the transition between life and spirit world

Myrrh
- Strengthens spirit
- Enhances visualization
- Enhances meditation
- Increases spiritual vibration
- Brings unconscious and shadows into the light
- Purifies
- Increases energy flow

Neroli
- Attracts positive energy
- Dispels worry
- Promotes clarity

Orange
- Increases joy and fun
- Supports abundance and prosperity in all things
- Strengthens romantic love

- Promotes harmony and balance

Patchouli
- It's an aphrodisiac
- Balances opposite energies (yin and yang)
- Promotes prosperity
- Dispels negativity
- Supports good dreams
- Harmonizes body and spirit
- Grounds

Peppermint
- Purifies
- Raises vibration
- Clears negativity
- Promotes healing of body, mind, and spirit
- Attunes you to psychic awareness
- Supports prosperity
- Causes prophetic dreams

Pine
- Cleanses and consecrates sacred spaces
- Cleanses crystals
- Provides psychic protection
- Supports manifestation and prosperity
- Dispels negativity

Rose
- Supports romantic love
- Raises vibration
- Balances opposite energies
- Balances body/mind/spirit
- Provides psychic protection
- Enhances psychic powers

Rosemary
- Purifies
- Provides protection against and transmutes negativity
- Cleanses the aura

- Prevents nightmares

Sage
- Transmutes or neutralizes negativity
- Cleanses the aura
- Provides psychic protection
- Activates Divine guidance system

Sandalwood
- Promotes spiritual well-being
- Helps you focus
- Raises vibration
- Enhances spiritual awareness
- Stimulates spiritual/energetic healing
- Activates Divine guidance system

Spearmint
- Cleanses aura and crystals
- Protects
- Assists with dreams
- Enhances focus and clarity

Star Anise
- Protects
- Purifies

Tea Tree
- Cleanses auras
- Purifies
- Balances upper chakras (heart through crown)

Thyme
- Promotes balance
- Enhances courage and inner strength

Valerian
- Grounds
- Relaxes
- Cats dig it

Vetiver
- Cleanses aura

- Protects
- Dispels phobias
- Assists in breaking negative patterns (habits, luck)
- Promotes prosperity

Yarrow

- Activates psychic abilities
- Promotes love
- Protects against negativity

Ylang Ylang

- Eliminates fear/worry
- Promotes self confidence
- Clears emotional and spiritual blockages

Herbs, Woods, and Resins

Herbs, woods, and resins have properties similar to those described above for the essential oils. You can use these–typically by burning them and spreading the smoke around–to cleanse and purify spaces. I wanted to mention a few of my favorite methods and materials here. I recommend getting a good book like *Cunningham's Encyclopedia of Magical Herbs* for specific uses of hundreds of herbs.

Sage

Burning sage has entered the mainstream thanks to the popularity of many paranormal and metaphysical television shows. From these media sources, most people understand burning sage can help clear negativity, and this is indeed true. Burning sage neutralizes energy completely, leaving an empty energetic vacuum. That means you need to fill the energy vacuum with another energy after burning the sage so you control what energy replaces what you've dispelled with sage. Any of the following burning herbs can replace the energy.

Typically, the way I use sage is like this: I have one

person walk with a sage smudge bundle (be sure you hold it over something to catch ashes) and wave the smoke around doors and windows and into closets and every corner of the house. Have another person walk behind following the same patters with another burning herb.

Palo Santo

Palo santo is a fragrant wood. It smells really good, and it is my favorite follow up to sage. It has the following properties:

- Grounding
- Promoting positive energy
- Raises vibration
- Activates Divine guidance
- Promotes calmness and soothes anxiety

Sweetgrass

Another burning herb that smells great, you will typically find sweetgrass in long braids. Light the end of the braid and allow it to smolder as you walk around the space. Sweetgrass purifies and promotes positive energy.

There are other substances you can burn to promote positive energy, as well, such as cedar or lavender. You can also refill the energy with essential oils.

Don't Forget to Smudge Yourself

Burning herbs, woods, and resins, sometimes called smudging, is most frequently used to cleanse spaces, but you can also smudge yourself. To do it, stand with your feet on the floor, arms spread wide. Have a person wave the smoke all around you, moving on all sides.

Chapter 14 – Energy Transfer/Energy Healing

There are many energy healing modalities that can assist with vibrational healing. In energy healing, another practitioner works with you and your body draws in the energy. You can learn various energy healing techniques and use them on yourself. For instance, as a Reiki practitioner and master, I apply Reiki to myself (and my pets!) every day, which helps me balance energy. There are numerous energy healing techniques you can learn for yourself or visit a practitioner who works with it. Below are brief descriptions of a few you can try.

If you have the opportunity to receive hands-on energy healing, I highly recommend it. It's a relaxing process that provides a way to care deeply for yourself.

Reiki

Reiki is a form of hands-on or distance energy healing. It is an ancient universal energy that comes from the universe through the practitioner, and the person receiving the Reiki draws it into his or her body. Reiki masters teach Reiki practitioners the philosophy and practice and then attune them to the energy so they can share it with others. Reiki level one practitioners are trained in hands-on Reiki. Reiki level two practitioners are taught how to use symbols and attuned to second level Reiki, which allows them to send Reiki across time and distance. Reiki masters are taught to attune others to Reiki, as well as how to teach it.

There are thousands of Reiki practitioners and masters. If this is a modality you are interested in, it is fairly easy to find a practitioner or to learn it yourself.

Quantum Touch®

Quantum Touch is another form of energy healing that can either be hands on or at a distance. Practitioners are trained by certified Quantum Touch trainers who have met the requirements of the course. The technique involves energy movement from the earth through breathing and works via entrainment (transferring vibration from the healer to the receiver). You can find QT practitioners through the website, QuantumTouch.com.

Emotional Freedom Technique (EFT)

EFT is an acupressure technique that involves tapping on various energetic points to release energy blockages. Through the use of tapping and positive affirmation, EFT can help with psychological healing. You can learn the basics of doing EFT for yourself at EFT.mercola.com.

Healing Touch

Healing Touch is another form of hands-on energy therapy that works with the body's magnetic field (biofield) to support emotional, spiritual, and physical health. Learn more about Healing Touch or find practitioners at HealingTouchProgram.com.

Homeopathy

Many people are surprised to learn homeopathy is a form of vibrational healing. Homeopathic substances work on the principle of like cures like. Taking a substance that, at full strength, can cause the same symptoms it is meant to treat, homeopathic medicines dilute the substance over and over until it doesn't retain any of the original substance, but instead the medicine contains the vibration of that substance. These substances then enter the body of the person taking them and vibrate at a frequency that helps to clear up the symptoms.

Homeopathy remedies are highly individual, so it's important to work with a trained homeopathic physician to ensure you take the right medication for your symptoms and condition.

Body Work

Various types of bodywork can also help raise vibration, create balance, and free energetic blockages. While it seems bodywork is just working on your physical body, remember it is impossible to separate body, mind, and spirit. Therefore, balancing the physical body can also facilitate balancing of energies.

It is possible for emotions and spiritual and mental pain to become trapped in the body, and when the patient experiences some type of bodywork, it releases that energy. I saw this firsthand when I worked in a chiropractic and massage therapy office for about eight years. I can't tell you how often I saw someone during the process of a physical treatment— either a spinal manipulation or deep tissue massage therapy— have a deeply emotional reaction following a treatment. People might start to laugh hysterically, cry, or anything in between as the physical manipulation released some primal energy that had been stored in their body.

I had a similar reaction once during a session of craniosacral therapy. One moment I was fine, and then next I was sobbing hysterically. Once the crying jag had passed, I felt lighter than I had in months. Something had been released inside of me.

Types of bodywork that can help with vibration include

but aren't limited to the following:

- Massage therapy and myofascial release
- Reflexology
- Chiropractic
- Craniosacral therapy
- Applied kinesiology
- Alexander technique
- Feldenkrais method
- Rolfing
- Hakomi

Acupuncture and Acupressure

There are many other physical forms of energy medicine that work with energy channels in the physical body. Acupuncture and acupressure are two of these. Both work with specific points in the meridians to clear blockages and allow energy to rebalance itself. Acupressure uses pressure on these points while acupuncture uses needles. You'll need to find practitioners trained in these techniques. A good place to start when locating them is through a local holistic health clinic.

Hypnotherapy

Hypnotherapy can also lead to vibrational balance and deep emotional, physical, and spiritual healing. Hypnotherapists have an array of tools at their disposal to help you uncover subconscious energy blocks and release them. I've had hypnotherapy several times, and every time I have come away spiritually, physically, and emotionally enriched.

During hypnotherapy, you are a state of deep relaxation where your conscious mind steps aside and your subconscious mind comes to the fore. During that period, you are deeply suggestible, so the hypnotherapist can offer posthypnotic suggestions to your subconscious that then activate in your waking life.

Many people fear hypnotherapy because they feel as if they are ceding control to someone else. However, it's important to understand even when your conscious mind has stepped aside, you are in control. A hypnotherapist cannot make you do anything you don't wish to, regardless of how suggestible your mind is when you are in a hypnotic trance.

Some of the ways a hypnotherapist can work with you follow.

Past Life Regression and Life Between Lives Regression Hypnotherapy

When we come into this life, we bring the energetic imprint of who we have been in our previous lives. Sometimes, this can cause us to slip out of energetic balance because we may have fears or phobias related to those previous lives, or we may carry karmic issues forward from previous lives.

Past life regression hypnotherapy offers the opportunity for you to see and understand how these past lives have come into your present life. Often, the understandings you glean from experiencing a past life in a trance state are all you need to release phobias, clear karmic issues, and rebalance your energetic systems.

Life between lives hypnotherapy takes you through death in a past life and into a state where you experience who you are when you are between lives. In other words, it allows you to experience, in a hypnotic state, who you are when you are your higher self. This is a very powerful experience that can give you insight into some of the circumstances you granted yourself in this lifetime (such as chronic health issues, your family of birth, other major life issues such as poverty or prosperity, etc.). From this higher perspective, you can suddenly understand this life you currently live as an embodied human and know for a fact you created your life and why you gifted yourself with certain circumstances.

This peek under the skirt of what we perceive as our 3-dimensional reality and into ultimate reality is a powerful and life-changing experience that allows you to approach your life from a much broader base of understanding. When you have these understandings, you can start to heal energetically.

I know this from direct experience because I've had several past life regression hypnotherapy sessions and a life between lives session. From those sessions, I came to understand how what I was being in this life was moving me in the direction of my life's purpose, and I was able to integrate lessons from previous lives into this one. It also shed light on several of my relationships, gifts, and challenges which have been invaluable as I have moved along my path.

For more information about past life regression hypnotherapy or life between lives hypnotherapy, check out Dr. Michael Newton's books *Journey of Souls* and *Destiny of Souls*, along with Brian Weiss's book *Many Lives, Many Masters*.

Sometimes regression therapy that regresses you in this lifetime can help, as well. It may help you understand pain from childhood trauma in a different way, for instance.

Hypnotherapy to Clear Blocks and Break Habits and Heal Physical Issues

Hypnotherapy can also help you deal with stubborn issues, health problems, and phobias. For example, my mother had hypnotherapy to work with her phobia of flying, and it helped tremendously. One of my hypnotherapists specialized in working with people who had habits they'd like to drop, such as smoking or overeating. By offering imagery and post-hypnotic suggestions, their clients are often able to move beyond phobias, habits that don't serve them, and many other issues.

When I went to see a hypnotherapist named Rita to help me with a health issue I was having, while I was in a trance she had me visualize my DNA in a beam of light being repaired so I was 100 percent whole and healthy. This was quite effective.

Other Modalities

Many other energy healing modalities exist. Please visit the websites below for more information.

- Pranic Healing – PranicHealingUSA.com
- Theta Healing – ThetaHealing.com
- Longevitology – Longevitology.org
- The Wonder Method – TheWonderMethod.com
- Brennan Healing Science – BarbaraBrennan.com
- Domancic Method of Bioenergy Healing – DomancicMethod.eu
- Polarity Therapy – PolarityTherapy.org
- Matrix Energetics – MatrixEnergetics.com

Chapter 15 – Food, Movement, and Body Image

It's no surprise that what you put in your body and how you move it affects your physical health, but food and movement are also important vibrational tools. Likewise, your body image can have a powerful affect on your vibrational rate and your ability to clear energetic imbalance.

You, The Body

When we get involved in spiritual pursuits, it's easy to ignore the body or think it isn't as important as our minds and spirits. However, your body is the one you have for this lifetime, and it's an important part of the trinity of body-mind-spirit. Each piece of that triad is just as important as the others in embodied humans, and each affects the others. So how you treat your body, how you think about it, and what you put into is paramount.

Body Image

Body image is a tricky thing. An article in *Glamour* magazine pointed out that about 97 percent of women at some point say they hate their bodies. Thoughts are creative, so imagine what the energy of body hate manifests. Not only can it harm the body energetically, but the belief we hate our body also causes us to treat it poorly in order to maintain some false ideal of beauty. Most often, we do this by underfeeding, over exercising, or both.

I'm at a pretty good place in my body image right now, but even so, I still notice old thoughts and comparisons popping into my mind. For example, when I participate in Nia classes, I can't help but notice in the mirrors how I compare to others. I am strong, healthy, and energetic. I can dance for hours at a time. I recently earned my Nia White Belt, which included 7 days of intensive movement and training. I can lift, create, and move well. I wake up every morning with fewer aches and pains than I've had in years.

My body does all I ask of it and more. It serves me beautifully but at times, I'm still hung up on how it looks because it is not the ideal. This is thinking I work every day to quash and replace so I can exist in a space of joy and gratitude, but it's a process. I can't remember a time when I didn't compare my body unfavorably to the ideal. Even when I was a size 2, I knew I was lacking something in the appearance of my body. Body image and comparison has always been background noise (and sometimes in the foreground) as part of my self-awareness. Intellectually, I know my body is magnificent, and I couldn't be happier with all it does for me. I'm taking the steps to have that knowledge move into my experience.

I can't help but wonder, though, what that constant negative dialog does to my body. What do you think its doing to yours? How much more amazing would our bodies be if we could eliminate the comparison to the ideal? How much more could we appreciate it, let go, and be in joy, which raises vibrations?

Our thoughts, words, and attitudes affect our outer experience. They affect our biology and physical expression. Masaru Emoto's messages from water confirm what negativity does to cellular structure. It begs the question, what are your negative thoughts about your body doing to it? How are they affecting it physically and energetically?

Every day, I'm grateful for what my body does for me, and I express that gratitude. However, throughout the day, insidious thoughts of dissatisfaction creep in, too – the ones that tell me because I am not the physical ideal, my body is somehow lacking. What are these conflicting thoughts doing to my body?

I know I am not alone in my body image struggles. I see it daily among friends, family, and even strangers on the street. Societal messages about our bodies lead us to think we are lacking. We feel ashamed when we fulfill the basic biological functions our body truly needs: eating and rest. We feel gratified when we push our bodies to a place where they are groaning in pain as we work out or our stomachs call out to us in hunger. Is this any way to treat something beloved? Would you push and judge someone you loved in such ways to force them to meet an unrealistic physical ideal?

Body image, negative self-talk, and comparison to an ideal are all bred into us from an early age and reinforced throughout our lives through various sources so we engage in various forms of self-abuse and self-torture because we do not meet that ideal.

How do we fix it? How do we heal? Awareness is an important first step. Listen to the thoughts you have and the words you speak about your body. Be in awareness, and when the negative thoughts about your body arise, stop them and replace them with words of gratitude.

What has your body done for you today? Did you sleep? Wake up? Breathe? Eliminate? Move? Think? Experience pleasure? Hear the signals of pain? This is your body, trying its hardest to partner with you, something it can't do if you continue to reject and malign it.

Listen to your body; it's talking to you. It's telling you something valuable. It's sending you signals, telling you what it needs, wants, likes, and doesn't like. All you have to do is listen and send it words of support, encouragement, and kindness which are the very things you would do for someone you love, so why not do them for yourself?

I decided a few years ago it was time to start partnering with my body instead of fighting it, and when I did things changed. I lost weight. I became more mobile. My pain levels decreased. My energy soared. A few years ago, I could barely move, but my partnership with my body has allowed me to move, dance, and experience joy and pleasure I haven't had since I was in my early 20s. Its an ongoing process, this partnership, and I admit I'm still not always the greatest partner because I have ongoing body image issues, but I'm working on it, and it is paying off.

This, then, isn't an admonishment to you. It's an invitation for you to ask your body what it needs and wants, to learn to speak and think to and about your body gently, kindly, and with gratitude. I'm inviting you to seek pleasure and be compassionate with yourself, and for you to enter into a partnership that can totally change your physical experience, if only you'll allow it.

Food

Along with writing about spirituality, vibrational healing, and metaphysics, I am a food and health writer. I've authored several cookbooks for people on special diets with everything ranging from vegan and paleo diets to diets for people with health conditions like GERD, IBS, inflammation, autoimmune disease, and hypothyroidism. Because of that, I'm intimately familiar with food and the many issues surrounding it.

We often have a lot of judgment when it comes to food. However, often the judgments about food focuses on how it makes us look (i.e. does it have too many calories so it's going to make us fat?) instead of how it makes us feel. I followed this approach for years, and I got sicker and sicker. It wasn't until I started focusing on how food made me feel that my health issues started to clear up and I lost weight. So instead of judging ourselves for eating food or for the foods we choose, we need to shift our focus to how food affects us vibrationally. It's important to understand the foods that work for me vibrationally might not work for someone else and vice versa. Your food choices are individual, and it's not up to me to judge how you eat or tell you what to eat. Food is neither good nor bad. It's just food. However, some foods may be more beneficial for you if you choose to achieve optimal physical and emotional health than others.

If you find you have judgments about food, such as classifying certain foods as "good" and others as "bad," it may be worthwhile to spend some time delving into your background to determine where you got the idea any food was good or bad. Journaling can help here.

New Rules for Food
When I talk to people about food and their diets, I often notice they have all sorts of rules they've created. Often these ideas come from media reports about what's good or bad for you, what's the best weight loss plan of the week, and a whole

smorgasbord of rules they've developed throughout their lives.

I spend hours a week combing through the latest studies about how food affects our bodies. Scientific writings break food down into its components—macronutrients (protein, fats, and carbs) and micronutrients (vitamins and minerals)—and the roles each of these play in our bodies. Science studies and explains how food affects weight and how it affects health. It explains how our bodies break down and digest the foods, how they store them as saved energy (fat) or use them for current energy. It studies how our bodies absorb nutrients and what it does with them.

Science is at least beginning to acknowledge the foods we eat affect our physiology, and then people like me share that information with others who are looking to affect some aspect of their biology, such as gaining or losing weight, lessening inflammation, or controlling certain health conditions through food.

Food is fuel, we are told. Use it wisely, and your body can't help but respond. Simple, right?

If it were that simple, everyone would be the picture of health. We would see food as fuel, eat the foods we need, avoid those we don't, and all experience optimum health. Since we don't and we aren't, clearly something else is going on, as well. How food affects us physically is an important part of the picture, but it's not the only part. To pretend food should merely be treated as fuel does everyone a disservice.

Humans are not like a simple gas-powered engine in which you pour the right amount of fuel and the engine performs. We are complex, multi-dimensional beings made up of far more than biology. We are body, mind, spirit, emotions, memories, conditioning, members of families and societies, and so much more. And food—which sciences suggests should merely be fuel—weaves itself throughout every one of these aspects of self, rendering it impossible to separate it into a simple biological component.

Close your eyes and think of a food from your childhood - one that you loved. How does it make you feel? I would guess that while there is a physical response, that is only part of the answer. Whatever food you are thinking of most likely has associations that are familial, cultural, emotional, and possibly even spiritual.

Food is deeply entrenched in every aspect of our lives. It is part of family celebrations and cultural traditions. We use it as reward and punishment. We connect it to abundance and scarcity. We use it in spiritual ceremonies and traditions. We use it to show love, generosity, and sharing. It serves as a way to gather socially. We use it for humanitarian purposes. Some control it in order to retain power. It can be used for social and behavioral conditioning. These are just a few of the many aspects of our lives in which food resides.

However, when we treat food as simply biological and fail to acknowledge the key position it occupies in mind, spirit, and emotions, we create a system in which people are most likely bound to fail in their goals about food. Food has to be more than fuel if we want to use to improve our health and create energetic balance. So people like me, who write about the health aspects of food, must find ways to make sure food continues to meet the mental, spiritual, and emotional needs of the individual, as well.

Food has to do more than just be biologically nutritious if we want to make a lasting change that affects health. In order to connect to eating for health, we also need to connect to the things that matter about the foods we eat. We need new "rules" about food in order to truly begin to nourish ourselves in the ways we need.

1. Start with Foods You Know Will Nurture You Physically

It still starts with food and selecting those that will help build your physical wellbeing. Choose the most nutritious, ethically raised, healthful ingredients available that you can afford. There's plenty of information available about what these foods are depending on physical health conditions and dietary needs. This is where you start, but it is important to go beyond just considering these foods as fuel.

2. Choose Foods that Please Your Senses

You eat with your all of your senses. Therefore, choose food that looks, tastes, and smells delicious. Consume foods with a satisfying balance of colors, textures, flavors, and aromas. Find foods with a delightful crunch or a satisfying slurp, or those that are pleasing to the eye and have your stomach growling before you take your first bite. Combine raw and cooked foods to vary texture and flavor. Cut foods into fun and interesting shapes. Use pretty garnishes. Balance the flavors of sweet, sour, bitter, salty, spicy, and umami.

3. Consume Foods from Cultural Traditions that Matter to You

Food is cultural. Therefore, it is essential to create and find nutritious foods from cultural traditions that matter to you. That doesn't just mean foods from your culture, but also from other cultural traditions that have meaning, or that you just love because they make darn good food. Use fresh herbs and spices to create a variety of flavor palates, such as the piquant and spicy Latin flavors, aromatic Asian flavors, or hearty, classic Western foods.

4. Choose Foods Connected to Good Memories

Food is tied to memory and comfort. Because of this, it is important to consume nutritious foods that are in some way similar to those you have eaten that have brought you joy in the past. They don't have to be exact replicas but rather have the essence of those other foods.

5. Choose Foods that Fit Within Your Ethical Framework

I've eaten a lot of different ways throughout my lifetime. I've been a vegetarian, a vegan, on the paleo diet, and several other diets, as well. So I am a true believer there is no "best" way for everyone to eat. There's only the best way for you, and I have no judgment about what someone deems acceptable in the foods they choose. The choice is always yours, and other issues, such as economics and availability, come into play.

However, with that being said, if at all possible, it's important to make food choices that fit within your ethical framework. If, for example, you believe no animal should sacrifice their life to feed you or supply you with any other things in your life, then follow a vegan diet. These are your ethics, and it's essential when working to balance your energy and raise your vibration that you live within your ethical framework. Likewise, it's important to consider other ethics when choosing foods as well. A few you may want to consider as you choose your foods follow.

If You Eat Animal Products, How Are They Raised?

Are they raised ethically and allowed to live as animals do, freely on green pastureland grazing on a natural diet or are they raised in factory farm operations where they stand shoulder to shoulder in their own manure, seldom moving more than a foot or two, given massive doses of antibiotics to stave off disease, and fed a grain-based diet that isn't healthy or beneficial for their species? The way your animal foods are raised leaves a vibrational imprint on the food you eat. While I'm not telling you which you should choose or which is better for you, and I fully understand the economics of affording certain foods over others, I would suggest that if foods raised this way offend your ethics, for your own vibrational health you make a different choice. There are more kindly raised animal proteins, such as free-range organic chicken eggs, that are much more affordable and still provide animal protein if that is important for you in your diet.

With Plant Based Foods, How Sustainably Are They Raised and How Do They Affect the Environment?

- Are the plants raised in giant factory-like monocultures that strip the earth of its minerals or in diverse gardens with multiple species that support one another and preserve nutrients the soil?
- Are they shipped on trucks for hundreds of miles before they reach your table or are they grown by local farmers?
- Does the money you pay for the food go to giant corporations or local independent farmers?
- Are pesticides sprayed on the plants that damage the soil and the environment?

- Are the seeds for the plants that make the foods genetically modified? For instance, are the seeds considered "roundup ready," meaning they are genetically engineered to resist the herbicide roundup so farmers can dump gallons of the stuff on their crops?

Again, I understand the economics involved in making ethical decisions with food, but if these are extremely important concerns for you, then it is worth considering making a different choice.

How Are the Foods Harvested, Prepared, and Packaged?
- Do they come in wasteful, non-recyclable, or non-biodegradable packaging?
- Do they contain all sorts of chemicals your body won't recognize as food?
- Are waste products of the manufacture harmful to the environment in some way?
- Are the raw materials for the food harvested on the backs of child or slave labor (such as some chocolate)?
- Are the foods Fair Trade so the people who produced them can get a fair share of the profits from the foods?

If these issues are important to you, then you'll need to consider whether your ethics allow consumption of these foods or if you need to skip them.

6. Skip the Foods that Have no Soul
It's easy to mindlessly eat something that has very little meaning or soul. Twinkies come to mind as the ultimate soulless food. There is no love there. Nobody lovingly prepared a Twinkie for you. It's a Frankenfood designed to be quick, sweet, and easy.

I'm not denying a Twinkie has its appeal, but does it have soul? There is nothing alive. There's nothing that will nourish you.

Nobody created soulless foods with the idea of nourishment in mind. They were created for one reason: profit. While it may taste good, does the food has soul? Ask yourself who has made it, and for what reason has this food been prepared. If the answer doesn't have to do with nourishment or some type of a personal connection, chances are it's not a food that's going to satisfy your mind, body, emotions, or spirit.

7. Prepare Foods with Consciousness and Intent

As you prepare your foods, do it with love for yourself and anyone else who will be consuming them. Intend, as you prepare the food, that its ingredients and nutrients will nurture you not only physically, but will also honor you emotionally, mentally, and spiritually.

8. Give Thanks

Food is spiritual; it's often used in spiritual ceremonies and rituals. Therefore, if food is part of your spiritual tradition (or even if it isn't), engage in a sense of spirituality and ritual when you eat. Before you eat, give thanks. If you eat animal proteins, honor the animal that provided the food. Give thanks to the Earth for supporting and nurturing the plant-based ingredients you are about to consume. Then, offer the intention the food will nourish your body and your spirit, matching or raising your spiritual vibration.

9. Eat Mindfully

Pay attention as you eat. Make eating an event and not something you do as you engage in another activity. Create a space for eating where you are not distracted (put down the smartphone! Turn off the television!) Eat mindfully, chew slowly, and allow yourself the full sensation of that which you are eating. Notice how the food smells, looks, and tastes. Pay attention to its texture as you chew and how it feels as it travels down your throat into your stomach.

More Than Fuel

It's time to acknowledge food is more than just fuel. To do anything else makes it difficult for us to truly allow foods to nourish us and support our overall health and wellbeing. Try these suggestions as you pursue good health through food to acknowledge the role food plays in all aspects of your being.

A Step-By-Step Approach to Finding What to Eat

Food philosophy aside, there is an effective way to determine how certain foods affect you, and which are best for your health or vibration. The process takes 30 to 60 days, but it's worthwhile if you feel your food choices may be affecting your overall health. Everyone has their own unique biology, so trying your buddy's diet that is so fabulous for him may not work for you.

I get emails all the time from people who read my cookbooks asking about some ingredient – whether they can have it, or why it is in the recipes. My response to the emails is always similar: It depends on your body. You need to take some time to discover how that ingredient affects you.

Over the years, I've tried all kinds of dietary approaches. Each approach brought changes – some for the better and some for the worse, but there wasn't a single dietary plan I followed that left me feeling as fantastic as I do right now.

Things changed when I personalized my diet,

discovering which foods nourished and supported my own unique biology, and which didn't.

While it takes time and some effort to personalize your diet, it can be done. The trick is to strip your diet bare for about 30 days (follow an elimination diet), and then slowly start adding foods back in to see how they affect you. Doing this can help you find the foods that best suit your vibrational needs. Always talk with your doctor before making a major dietary change.

Step One: Learn to Listen to Your Body
Before you start, it's important you learn to listen to your body's signals. Keep a journal of food, activity, and how you feel. It doesn't need to be complicated – just write everything you consume, write your activity, and note if you feel energized, sleepy, sore, irritable, hungry, cranky, or any other physical or emotional symptoms and feelings. As you do this, you may notice patterns emerge after you eat certain foods.

This journaling does something else, as well. It teaches you to tune into the signals your body is sending. It teaches you physical, mental, and emotional symptoms aren't just "normal" variations, but that they are messages from your body to you. Listening is the first step.

Step Two: Learn What to Eliminate
In the elimination diet, you'll be removing foods that may cause reactions. It's a big list, but bear in mind you won't necessarily need to eliminate all of it forever. Rather, you'll eliminate it for about 30 days and then slowly add things back in to see what your body tolerates. Here's a list:

Processed Foods

This includes pretty much anything in a bag, box, or package. A partial list:

- Cookies, crackers, chips, and snack foods
- Pasta and pre-made pasta sauces
- Candy
- Pre-made foods or food mixes, such as Rice-a-Roni
- Fast food
- Baked goods like bread, donuts, cakes, and pies
- Canned pre-made foods like chili, soup, pasta sauce (with the exception of organic broth)
- Foods that have long lists of things you can't pronounce, such as preservatives, artificial colors and flavors, binders, and emulsifiers
- Protein bars
- Meal replacement shakes

Dairy Products

This includes both fermented and non-fermented dairy, including:

- Milk
- Cheese
- Ice cream
- Yogurt
- Kefir

Soy

This includes all forms of soy including:

- Tofu
- Edamame
- Soybean oil
- Soymilk

Grains

All grains including (but not limited to):

- Rice
- Quinoa
- Wheat
- Oats
- Bulgur
- Barley

Nuts

All nuts including but not limited to:

- Peanuts (which are actually legumes)
- Walnuts
- Pine nuts
- Pecans
- Cashews
- Almonds
- Hazelnuts
- Brazil nuts
- Pistachios
- Nut butters

Sugars and Sweeteners

All sugars and sweeteners with the exception of stevia. This includes but is not limited to:

- Sugar
- Honey
- Molasses
- Maple syrup
- Corn syrup
- High-fructose corn syrup
- Rice syrup
- Aspartame (NutraSweet)
- Sucralose (Splenda)
- Saccharine
- Acesulfame-K (acesulfame potassium)
- Sugar alcohols like erythritol, xylitol, and others

Nightshades
These are fruits and veggies that include:

- Potatoes (white, not sweet)
- Tomatoes
- Eggplant
- Bell peppers
- Chili peppers
- Tomatillos
- Goji berries

Legumes
This includes but is not limited to:

- Beans (with the exception of green beans)
- Lentils
- Peanuts
- Soybeans and edamame
- Peas
- Chickpeas

Industrial Seed Oils and Hydrogenated Fats
This includes but isn't limited to:

- Soybean oil
- Canola oil
- Corn oil
- Vegetable oil
- Peanut oil
- Cottonseed oil
- Shortening
- Margarine
- Safflower oil
- Grapeseed oil

Gluten
Gluten is sneaky. It's obviously in gluten-grains like wheat, barley, rye, and some oats, but it also shows up in

unexpected places, like:

- Soy sauce (unless specifically labeled gluten-free)
- Mustards (read labels)
- Malt
- Beer
- Soups, sauces, and gravies
- Imitation crab
- Restaurant scrambled eggs and omelets

Beverages

While you're in the elimination phase, your best bet is to consume water. Avoid other beverages, including:

- Juice
- Lite beverages (like Crystal Light)
- Regular and diet soda
- Energy drinks
- Coffee (except decaf)
- Tea (except herbal)
- Alcoholic beverages

Step Three: Plan to Eliminate

Next, it's time to plan. By nature, I'm not a planner, so this step is not an easy one for me. If you are a planner, however, you're going to be in heaven! It's time to get organized.

Stock Your Pantry

Stock your fridge and pantry with the foods you'll be eating over the next 30 days. While it may vary for you, these are the foods I recommend on an elimination diet.

Organic Veggies

If you can get seasonal produce, even better! If you're a vegan, fruits, veggies, seeds, herbs, and spices will be your life's blood for the next few weeks. Stock your fridge with veggies, such as:

- Dark leafy greens like spinach and kale
- Cruciferous veggies like cauliflower, broccoli, and cabbage
- Root veggies like onions, beets, and carrots
- Other green veggies like asparagus and artichokes
- Sweet potatoes
- Summer and winter squash, including acorn, butternut, zucchini, spaghetti, and patty pan squashes
- Mushrooms

Organic Fruit

Stock your fridge and pantry with low-glycemic, organic fruits, such as:

- Avocado
- Berries (except goji, as noted above)
- Lemons and limes
- Apricots
- Peaches
- Nectarines

Animal Proteins

If you can find them, choose organic, pastured sources of animal protein, including:

- Eggs
- Poultry
- Wild-caught fish
- Wild-harvested shellfish and mollusks
- Beef
- Lamb
- Organ meats
- Pork

Herbs and Spices

Herbs and spices will help bring flavor to your foods.

These include, but aren't limited to:

- Cinnamon
- Allspice
- Nutmeg
- Cloves
- Ginger and ginger root
- Cumin
- Turmeric
- Coriander
- Oregano
- Tarragon
- Basil
- Parsley
- Thyme
- Garlic
- Sea salt
- Pepper

Expeller Pressed Oils and Unprocessed Fats

The goal with fats and oils is to find those that aren't refined through an industrial process. Good choices include:

- Avocado oil
- Extra-virgin olive oil
- Extra-virgin coconut oil
- Macadamia oil (expeller pressed)
- Duck fat
- Lard
- Tallow

Flavorings

Your diet doesn't have to be flavorless. You can add some of the following flavorings:

- Citrus zest
- Vinegars (with the exception of malt)

- Dijon mustard (read ingredients)
- Mustard powder
- Salsa (check ingredients)
- Coconut milk
- Organic broth

Seeds

You can also use seeds, such as:

- Chia
- Flax
- Pumpkin
- Sesame
- Sunflower

If possible, remove temptations from your kitchen. If it's not possible to get rid of all the processed foods, then at least keep them in their own separate spot so you don't see them and aren't tempted by them.

Step 4: Enlist Support

Let your family and friends know what you are doing and why. Explain you are working to find a diet that works for you so you can be in good health. Ask them to please not try to tempt you with foods outside of your elimination diet.

Step 5: Eliminate for 30 Days

Once you're ready, get started. Eat only the allowed foods for a full 30 days. Give yourself that time to clear your body of any substances it doesn't respond well to. Don't worry about counting calories or macronutrients. Eat when you're hungry, drink lots of water, get plenty of sleep, and engage in gentle exercise as your body allows.

Step 6: Journal

During the 30 days, keep a journal, noting what you eat

and your symptoms. Note positive changes. Please note in the first week or so of the elimination, you may feel a bit worse as the toxins work their way out of your body although some people notice an immediate change for the better. Stick with it for the full 30 days.

Step 7: Re-introduce Foods One at a Time

After your 30 days, you can start to reintroduce foods and food groups. It's important to do this one food at a time so you can note how it feels in your body. To reintroduce:

1. Choose a single food from one of the eliminated groups, such as cheese.
2. Eat a little bit of cheese (an ounce or so). Wait 24 hours, noting any symptoms.
3. If you have symptoms, no more cheese (or whatever food it is).
4. If you don't have symptoms, eat a little more of the food at a couple meals.
5. Watch for the symptoms again. If you have them, stop. That food isn't compatible with your body.
6. If no symptoms, then try another food from the same group. So if you're having dairy, try a little yogurt.
7. Wait 24 hours. If symptoms, that food group probably isn't your friend and you'll want to avoid it.
8. If no symptoms, spend the next week trying other foods from the food group and noting any symptoms. If you don't have any, you can assume that food group is compatible with your body. If you do have symptoms, note which foods from the group cause them and avoid those.
9. Repeat after a week or two with the next food group.

Using this process, you'll gradually get a picture of which foods work with your own unique biology, and you can adapt your diet accordingly.

The 90/10 Principle

Once you've got it all dialed in, you can begin to make choices that will help you attain better health. Once I did that, I started using what I call the 90/10 principle. I try to eat cleanly (that is, with foods that don't affect me) 90 to 95 percent of the time. Occasionally, I may allow myself certain foods, such as a little sucralose, dairy, or an alcoholic beverage. There are some foods, however, that I consider deal-breakers (I never eat them) because they have such a negative effect on my body. Your deal breakers may be different than mine, but mine include:

- Gluten (I have celiac disease)
- Sugars of any kind (I'm super carb-intolerant and the weight just piles on – and I'm a sugar junkie, so a little triggers my cravings and desire for a "fix")
- Fast and processed foods
- Grains (same reason – carb intolerance)

Tips

The following tips can help you:

- Drink tons of water to flush out toxins.
- Engage in gentle exercise.
- Listen to your body and heed its signals.
- Don't skip the food/symptoms journal. It's easy to forget when you're feeling well, how poorly you felt before.
- Get plenty of rest and sleep.
- Talk to your primary health care provider before you start any new food or exercise program.
- Have patience with yourself. If you slip, start over.

Remember you're seeking what works for you, not for somebody else. You are creating a sustainable, lifetime eating plan that supports and nurtures your good health.

Worth the Effort

The process is involved, but well worth it. I hear from a lot of people who follow an elimination diet and reap the benefits of better health, fewer symptoms, and more vitality. This isn't about weight loss. It's about creating a healthy environment within your body where you can thrive in the best health possible.

Food for the Chakras

Eating certain foods can help balance different chakras. In general, choose foods with colors that match the chakra colors. Some foods for each are listed below.

Root Chakra

- Cherries
- Pomegranate
- Beets
- Tomatoes
- Strawberries
- Raspberries
- Red bell pepper
- Radish

Sacral Chakra

- Carrots
- Orange
- Tangerine
- Sweet potato
- Squash
- Orange bell pepper

Solar Plexus Chakra

- Golden beets
- Yellow squash
- Spaghetti squash
- Yellow bell pepper

- Banana

Heart Chakra
- Kale
- Spinach
- Green apples
- Swiss chard
- Avocado
- Parsley
- Bok choy
- Cabbage

Throat Chakra
- Blackberries
- Blueberries
- Purple potatoes

Third Eye Chakra
- Eggplant
- Purple grapes
- Purple cabbage
- Purple kale
- Purple carrots

Crown Chakra
- Mushrooms
- Onions
- Potatoes
- Pears
- Endive

Other Substances

I'll preface this section by saying that what you choose is up to you. However, the following substance recommendations are those that are the most beneficial for your vibrational health.

Water

Drink plenty of pure water. Filtered and non-fluoridated

is best if you have it available. Try to have at least 64 ounces per day, especially when you are working on vibrational healing. Water will help you eliminate any toxins that move into your body from the process. Water is also an important part of your life force. It's helpful to avoid water stored in plastic bottles that can leach toxins into it.

Caffeine

Caffeine is a drug and a mind-altering addictive substance. I say this without judgment given I am a caffeine addict on and off and have been over the years. Still, it's best that you minimize caffeine, which can throw the body out of balance by stressing adrenal glands and promoting anxiety.

Intoxicants

Intoxicants include any alcohol or drugs that alter brain function. I understand using alcohol to relax. I've been known to have a glass of wine or bourbon from time to time, and I occasionally will use narcotic medications when I have a migraine. However, these mind-altering substances consumed on a regular basis lower vibration and create vibrational imbalances. If you feel you must drink or use mind altering substances daily, it's important you examine why this is so because an energetic imbalance is likely.

Tobacco

Tobacco is a personal choice, but from a vibrational standpoint it is harmful. It's up to you whether you use it, but if you are addicted to tobacco, it may be worthwhile to determine what type of imbalance is at play to fuel your addiction.

Prescription and OTC Drugs

I am of the opinion prescription drugs are grossly overprescribed and OTC medications are overused. However, I am not a doctor and am unqualified to make any medical recommendations. If you are concerned about medications you take, I recommend a discussion with your primary health provider. Remember herbs are a form of medication, as well. Talk with your doctor about any herbal substances you take.

Vitamins and Supplements

Ideally, the best source of vitamins and minerals comes from eating a varied and nutritious diet containing whole foods. However, some people are unable to do this, and others may have nutrient deficiencies. It's not my place to recommend whether you should take nutritional supplements. If you do, make sure they come from natural sources and are not synthetic. Synthetic vitamins and minerals are more likely to deepen vibrational imbalances because your body doesn't recognize them as a substance it would normally consume.

Movement

There's no doubt exercise is beneficial for the body. It has tremendous health benefits, and a healthy body can affect energetic balance. Some types of exercise even have a spiritual and meditative aspect to them, making them great for your overall energetic balance. However, it's important you learn to listen to your body and engage in movement forms that sustain it instead of breaking it down. If you're an exerciser that believes in *no pain, no gain*, then you may be doing more harm than good.

Nine Joyful Forms of Exercise for High Vibration

When I was a 20-something, I'd beat my body into submission with hours of grueling weight training, running, and cardio equipment. While I liked how the exercise felt when I was done, there was something joyless about it. I didn't love it. I didn't even really like it. But I did it day after day because I felt I had to. It became just another thing I had to do, instead of something I looked forward to doing.

I also believe it played a role in developing 25 years of autoimmune disease that caused me to gain weight and rendered me unable to work out. During those years of heavy exercise, I failed to heed my body's signals. I believed in the mantra, "No pain, no gain," and I worked myself past exhaustion and pain in pursuit of a physical ideal. There was no joy, just work as I grudgingly rose at 4:30 every morning to get to the gym for hours of exercise.

Then I was ill for 25 years. I developed exercise intolerance. When I worked out, my body rebelled, and I was left feeling even sicker and more pain-ridden than if I didn't exercise at all. I was trapped in a downward spiral, all because I failed to listen to my body's request for activities that brought pleasure and joy instead of pain and drudgery.

I'm not saying that for everyone, conventional workouts are drudgery. I know many people who love weight lifting, cross-fit, cardio machines, and similar exercises. If these workouts bring you joy, then by all means keep them as a part of your life.

However, what if you're like me, and you don't really like it? What if your body is sending you signals begging you to engage in activity that brings you pleasure and allows you to experience joy? What if you found a workout you loved so much you couldn't wait to get to it another session, and another, and another?

For me, finding those joy-filled workouts has been just

the key for regaining my health. While I encourage you to seek your own joy in finding unconventional forms of exercise, I offer a few suggestions as a place to start.

#1: Nia

This is the workout that brought me back into daily movement. It's a combination of dance, playing like a kid, martial arts, and many other forms of exercise. Nia, which you take in a class (or you can order videos) emphasizes working the body's way, tailoring movements to your own level, bringing your own style of dance to the routines, and experiencing the pleasure and joy of movement. It's also a great cardio and strengthening workout, and I love the way it feels in my body and my soul.

#2: Belly Dance

For a few months, I took tribal belly dance classes, and I loved it. The movement comes from learning to isolate muscle groups, and it's great for your core muscles. It's also all about women dancing together and engaging in the Divine feminine, so for me there's a lot of joy associated with it. Plus, you get to dress up in cute, swishy hip scarves that jingle.

#3: Swinging

I'm talking about the kind you did when you were a kid — not spouse swapping. Head to the park and hop on a swing set. Pump your legs to go as high as you can. It's great for the core, and it feels freeing and fabulous.

#4: Dancing – of Any Kind

While I list tribal belly dance and Nia separately, I think any kind of dancing is a wonderful workout. Sign up for ballroom dance classes or salsa lessons with your partner. Turn on music and dance around the house in your underwear. Go out dancing with friends. Just move. To music. It feels fantastic, joyful, freeing, and fun.

#5: Sports

It doesn't matter if it's tennis, racquetball, ping pong, kickball, basketball, dodgeball, or any other sport. Find a sport you love and participate. Join a recreation league. Run around like you did when you were a kid.

#6: Playing

Remember when you were a kid and you'd play Frisbee, roll down hills, climb on the monkey bars, spin in circles, fly kites, ride bikes, roller skate, and dozens of other activities that were fun and allowed you to blow off steam? What's stopping you as an adult? Take time every day to engage in active play – with your kids, with your dogs, with friends, with family, or even by yourself. Move with joy, and your body will respond. So will your spirit.

#7: Hiking

Get outside and move. In nature. While appreciating nature. Taking local hikes or walks is a great way to gently encourage your body to move.

#8: Water Sports

Whether you're kayaking, canoeing, waterskiing, swimming, or rowing a boat, you're exercising. But it's so much fun, you hardly realize what you're doing. Water sports are great exercise that can also provide you with moments of Zen if you remain present time focused in what you're doing.

#9: Biking, Skating, and Scooting

Whether it's a skateboard, scooter, inline skates, bicycle, unicycle, or long board, if you're making something with wheels and no engine move, you're getting a great workout.

Just Move

What's the trick to bringing joy to your exercise routine? Just move. Move while it feels good in ways that feel good in your body. When your body tells you it's time, stop. If your body wants to work harder, play harder, slowing down or stopping as your body signals you it's ready. By finding activities you love, you can give your body all the exercise it craves without needing to engage in workouts that feel like work.

Gentle Movement for People in Pain

When you're in pain, the thought of exercising can be difficult. However, these gentle forms of exercise meet you where you are and through a process of slow, gentle movement that allows you to adapt for your own needs, reintroduces exercise into your life. This can help you grow stronger and more mobile. Some great gentle exercise forms follow. Always talk with your doctor before starting a fitness or movement program.

Tai Chi

If you've seen people moving slowly and gracefully on a sunny day in the park, chances are you've seen Tai Chi in action. The movements are completed in slow motion, and they appear to be a beautiful and graceful dance. This ancient Chinese martial art can improve balance, mobility, agility, and flexibility and provide cardiovascular and muscular strengthening and endurance benefits. For people in severe pain, you can start sitting doing just arm movements. As you progress, you can do it for longer periods and add additional movements.

Restorative Yoga

Restorative yoga isn't as challenging or bendy as its

more vigorous cousins. In fact, it's quite gentle. Classes usually feature slow, easy poses sustained for long periods, so you may only complete 5 to 10 poses (usually seated and lying poses) in an hour class. Instructors encourage the use of props (such as straps and blocks) to assist with asanas (poses) and can offer modifications to people who need them. The classes strengthen and aid in flexibility and relaxation.

Many yoga studios offer restorative classes. You can also find restorative yoga online, but if you are dealing with chronic pain I strongly recommend working with a teacher trained to help you adapt poses to meet your own needs.

Nia Moving to Heal
Nia Moving to Heal is another class that features slow, gentle movements that can be adapted to your individual level. Classes can be done in a chair if needed, as well. The movements strengthen, improve flexibility and mobility, improve agility, and offer cardiovascular benefits. The teachers are trained in assisting people with the movements and adapting them to individual needs. Many Nia studios offer Moving to Heal. Visit NiaNow.com to find classes in your area.

Foundation Training
Foundation training is designed to allow you simple and effective movements to help you combat pain, particularly back pain. The gentle movements strengthen the muscles of the core to help prevent future injuries, as well. For more information, visit FoundationTraining.com.

Swimming and Water Aerobics
Swimming and water aerobics are non-impact, so they are easier on your body, which makes them ideal for people in pain. Engaging in these forms of exercise can improve

cardiovascular endurance, flexibility, mobility, muscle strength, muscle endurance, and agility.

Walking

The great thing about walking is you can do it at your own pace and go the distance that is comfortable for you. Walk at a comfortable pace and only go as far as feels good in your body. Walking will increase mobility, cardiovascular endurance, and muscular endurance.

Movement Specifically Designed to Balance Energy

Some forms of movement are designed to facilitate the movement of energy (qi or prana) through your body in order to achieve balance.

Yoga

Yoga can be gentle or difficult. It can be calming or stimulating. It can be peaceful or active. Yoga wears many faces depending on the type taught and the instructor. However, all of it facilitates the movement of energy throughout your body as you engage in asanas (poses). You can adapt yoga for injuries, as well. It strengthens muscles, improves cardiovascular and muscular endurance, improves mobility, and increases flexibility. It also helps relieve stress and encourages inner peace.

While most people think of yoga as simply a form of movement (asanas), yoga also includes meditation (called dyana), pranayama (breathing), having an ethical view of the world (called yama), an attitude of self-discipline and kindness toward self (called niyama), an attitude of self-awareness (called pratyahara), focus and concentration (called dharana), and merging with the oneness (called Samadhi).

Asanas for the Chakras

There are multiple asanas that stimulate each chakra. A few are listed below.

- Root chakra –mountain pose, warrior two
- Sacral chakra – Pigeon or double pigeon pose, happy baby pose, frog pose
- Solar plexus chakra – warrior II, plank, child's pose, corpse pose
- Throat chakra – shoulder stand, supported fish pose, legs on wall pose
- Third eye chakra – sun salutation, child pose, downward dog
- Crown chakra – tree pose, supported headstand

Martial Arts

There are numerous forms of martial arts that focus on defensive movements, offensive strikes, discipline, and the movement of life force energy, called qi or chi, throughout the body. I recommend finding a practice that speaks to you, because if it calls to you, it is likely you need that form of energy in your life.

Qigong

Qigong is an ancient Chinese movement form. It focuses on controlled breathing and movement exercises (similar to Tai Chi), as well as meditation. The focus of qigong is mastering your energy.

Mudras

Mudras seem simple, but using them can open energy flow throughout your body. Mudras involve hand and arm positions that foster energy flow. You can perform the following mudras for each chakra. During meditation, you can hold each mudra for three to five minutes while focusing on the corresponding chakra.

Root Chakra

This mudra focuses on grounding, the earth element, and stimulating the root chakra. To perform the mudra:

1. Lay your hands in your lap with your palms facing up and the backs resting on your legs.
2. With the thumb and forefinger, touch the tips together, making a circle (like signaling okay). Don't lift the hands, and keep the other fingers extended.

Sacral Chakra

This mudra has the element of water and its focus is on emotional intimacy and connection to the all. It stimulates the second chakra. To perform it:

1. Lay your left hand in your lap with your arm parallel to the front plane of your body (elbow at a 90-degree angle). Cup the left hand near your belly button with the palm facing up.
2. Mirror the gesture with your right hand, placing the back of your right hand in the palm of your left.

Solar Plexus Chakra

This mudra aligns with the element of fire and the third chakra. It stimulates self-esteem and self-worth. To perform it:

1. Hold your arms with your elbows at your sides, your forearms extended so they are perpendicular to the front of your body.
2. Place your hands, palms together in prayer position with your fingers pointing directly away from the body at solar plexus height.

Heart Chakra Mudra

For this mudra, use just your left hand, held at heart height. It aligns with the element of air and supports the heart chakra. To perform it:

1. Hold the thumb and forefingers of your right hand in a circle with the tip of the thumb touching the tip of the middle finger and holding the other fingers curled in the circle, as well.
2. Place the fingertips against the center of your chest with the back of your hand facing away from your chest but parallel to it.

Throat Chakra Mudra

This mudra aligns with sound and the throat chakra. Hold it at throat height. To perform the mudra:

1. Hold your right and left hands in the shape of a C with your arms hanging at your sides, thumbs up and fingers curled into the C with knuckles facing downward.
2. Now bring both hands up. Place the cupped fingers of the left hand on top of the cupped fingers of the right hand and allow the thumbs to touch. You will be making a big O shape with both hands.
3. Hold this in front of the throat.

Third Eye Chakra Mudra

This mudra represents time and aligns with the third eye chakra. It stimulates psychic vision and intuition. To perform the mudra:

1. Place your hands in prayer position, fingertips facing up.
2. Press the pads of the thumbs (where your thumbprints are) together and point the thumbs down. This will pull the palms of your hands apart so your hands will only be touching at fingertips and thumbs.

3. Fold down the pointer and middle fingers so the fingernails and knuckles touch each other. Your ring finger and pinky will still be extended and touching on the pads of the fingertips (where the fingerprints are).
4. Hold the mudra up in front of your third eye chakra.

Crown Chakra Mudra

This mudra aligns with your crown chakra and the element of space. It supports Divine communication. To perform it:

1. Clasp your hands together with your fingers intertwined. When hands are clasped, your right hand is the bottom hand and your left hand is the top hand, so your right thumb will fold below your left thumb.
2. Extend the pinkies straight up so the fingertip pads are touching while keeping the rest of the fingers clasped. Hold up to your crown chakra.

Chapter 16 – Vibrational Healing for the Planet

I suspect we can all agree there's some messed up stuff happening in the world today. Heck, there's probably some messed up stuff happening in your personal life because that's just the way life is sometimes. The thing is, it can be difficult to stay in that happy, vibey, spiritual place when things are happening that don't seem to fit with a happy, vibey, spiritual worldview. I get it.

I have a lot of friends who are upset at world events right now, and I can see why they feel that way. I admit to having some anxiety arise myself. The news is full of items that seem designed to jack up our blood pressure and fill us with fear.

Old Energy Pushing Back

I believe humanity is changing for the better. I believe people are raising their vibration and therefore raising the vibration of the planet. I believe we are living in a time of new energy and headed towards a better world as a species. And I also believe that right now, the old energy is pushing back, and it's pushing hard. I also believe we have a choice. We can live in fear and contribute to the old energy, or we can try to the best of our ability to live in love so the vibration of the planet continues to rise and eventually the old energy will no longer have any power.

Choose Love

As much as possible, I choose to live in love. With that said, it doesn't mean I am passively accepting this pushback of the old energy. I care passionately about social justice, the welfare of others, our planet and its health and environment, and many other issues, and I do every loving thing in my capacity to forward those causes. However, I'm trying my best not to live in fear about current events, and I'm trying my best not to contribute to the angry, fearful, divisive, hateful rhetoric. Hate never cures hate. Fear never cures fear. Anger never cures anger. When we add our own negative emotions to a cesspool of other negative emotions, all we do is make it stronger and lower our own vibration in the process. And I don't believe species human on planet Earth needs to take a big step backwards because the old energy is pushing back.

You have a choice how you respond, and you can respond even more passionately with love than you can with anger, hate, or fear. I invite you if you feel passionately about an issue to work hard to forward it, but I also recommend you do it with love in your heart. I ask that you keep your vibration high and your energy balanced and don't give in to hate, anger, or fear. You can still just as passionately work for a cause without those low vibration emotions. In fact, working for a cause from a place of love and peace brings more power to your work, and it's more likely to attract others to your cause, as well.

As someone who is working to balance your energy, you are in a unique position of holding vibration for the planet and of helping others to see through your own example of peace, joy, and determined action in times of turmoil how they, too, can find a positive way to make a difference.

Healing the Planet

The only way we are going to heal the planet is by

raising the vibration of the whole, and the only way we can do that is if we each hold our own integrity and high vibration no matter what is happening in the world. When something happens that comes from pain, fear, the need to control, or other low-vibration energies, we need to respond with love and compassionate action. You can do this by compassionately and lovingly support causes that matter to you, and by sending love and vibration to people existing in the old energy, as well as to situations that arise or to the entire planet.

A Meditation for Sending Healing

Whenever you find yourself getting upset at the actions of people in government, world leaders, jerks, violent people, criminals, or any others, you can use this meditation. You can also use it when calamities occur, such as natural or human caused disasters. It's a wonderful all-purpose meditation that sends love and healing where it is needed while also helping you stay focused in love no matter what has happened.

1. Sit or lie comfortably with your eyes closed and your hands in your lap with your palms facing up. Breathe deeply.
2. When you feel peaceful and relaxed, imagine someone you love. This needs to be someone who truly makes your heart sing. Picture that person (or pet) and allow yourself to feel love and joy bubbling up inside.
3. Bring that love into your heart as you notice your heartbeat. Feel the love grow as it sits in your heart chakra, and feel your heartbeat pumping all of that love through your body. Feel it permeate every cell and every strand of DNA in your body. See yourself glowing with the light of love so much it is pouring out of your pores. While the light fills your body, direct part of it to your hands and allow it to stream from your hands and into the world.

4. Now, maintaining the feeling of love, bring the person, place, situation, or even the entire planet into the light that is filling your heart. Put them there and allow the light to surround them.

5. As you do this, offer an affirmation for healing. For example, for a world leader you might affirm, "May you have the strength and courage to govern in a manner that serves the highest and greatest good of humanity." If it's healing for a person, a group of people, or a situation you might affirm, "The light of love surrounds you and provides healing for your greatest and highest good." Ask your Divine guidance system to help you come up with the perfect affirmation. Stay in the energy of love while you do this.

6. Hold the person or situation in the light of love for as long as feels comfortable. Then release it saying, "I give thanks, I let it be so, and so it is." Send them away from the beams of light on your hands. As they fade off into the distance, see the light still surrounding them. Now, stop the light from streaming from your hands and feel the love coursing through your body and surrounding you once again. Affirm, "I am safe, I am love, I am peaceful." Or whatever feels right to you.

7. When you are ready, give thanks to the universe, say, "Let it be so," and open your eyes.

The Vibration of Empowerment

It's a personal choice which of the tools I've provided you choose to use in your life to facilitate energetic balance. After all, everything in life comes down to a personal choice, and only you can decide which tools will work best for you given where you feel you'd like to go with your spiritual, mental, and emotional wellness. Your Divine guidance system is poised and ready to help you choose those tools that empower you on your spirit's path in this embodied lifetime.

The process of vibrational healing isn't always easy, but it's always worthwhile and often a joyful and enlightening experience. The higher you vibrate and the more you balance your energy, the more balance and higher vibration you bring to the planet. And just by vibrating a little higher and being a little more balanced, you also then become a tool of healing for people around you as their vibration entrains to yours.

It can be difficult to learn things about yourself, particularly as you uncover shadows you've kept hidden even from yourself. I understand. It's an ongoing process for me, as well. You're not alone on the path. We all are there beside you at various stages of our learning and self-discovery. However, now you have new tools that can help, should you choose to use them.

Regardless of what you discover about yourself in the process, there's something important to remember. You are Divine. Every part of you is a piece of Divinity walking around in a human body. Your magnificence crosses the universe and fills its every nook and cranny with deep beauty and love. And though you may uncover some surprises along the way as you shake of layers of conditioning and misunderstanding, nothing you discover can take away the fact your substance is Divine, and your true nature is love.

It's like polishing a diamond covered in layers of rocks and dirt. You may chip away at it for hours, days, weeks, months, or years. With each layer you remove, you find another, and another, and another. However, underneath lies something beautiful and valuable that peeks through a little more with each layer.

You are that diamond. Sure there's a little dirt covering parts, but we all have it. However, the more you work at it, the more the diamond sparkles through until there it is in all its glory, casting the light of the universe on everyone and everything. Shine on, beautiful diamond.

Acknowledgements

Several months ago I had a tarot reading with the fabulous Jennifer Lucero Earle. During the reading, Jennifer and I discussed this book, which had been sitting inside of me awaiting its birth. However, I felt I wasn't quite ready yet, but I wasn't sure why. That day, Jennifer and I discussed what I needed to do to bring this book to light. It turns out I did exactly as we discussed and lo and behold, here it is. So first I'd like to thank Jennifer for the magic, because she helped me find the path from there to here.

Next, I always need to express my thanks to my husband Jim who suffers from ignored husband syndrome whenever I write a book. I write a lot of books, so it happens more than I'd like to admit. But he's always supportive and always a good sport. I'd also like to thank him for proofreading. It's a good thing he has an eye for detail because I don't. Thanks also to the kids (my kids), Tanner and Kevin, who tolerate their mom/stepmom writing about them in pretty much every single book ever.

I've had a lot of teachers over the years who have taught me things I've assimilated and used in some form or another in my writing and teaching. Particular thanks to some recent teachers who have helped a lot, including my alchemy teachers Ashley Barrett and Michaela Rand, my energy healing teacher Howard Batie, my psychic mentor Seth Michael, and my Nia moms Laurie Bass and Christina Wolf. I'd also like to thank my students, because I learn just as much from them as they do from me (and maybe more!)

Thanks to the people who have been reading the manuscript for me to give me an idea of whether I'm on the right track including Josh Barber, William Becker, Jennifer Smith-Brooking, Barbara Sudar, Elizabeth Wise Mazak, and Ashley Barrett.

Thanks to everyone with input on the cover art. Special mentions go to Jayme Tomasek for the photo, and Tristan David Luciotti, Amy Castellano, and to Jan Andrade for the design inspiration.

And to my tribe who offer feedback, support, and all sorts of other stuff, thank you to you all. There are a lot of you, and I'm afraid I'll miss someone if I name names. You know who you are, and I love you.

About the Author

Karen Frazier is the author of paranormal, metaphysical, and energy healing books including *Avalanche of Spirits: The Ghosts of Wellington, Dancing with the Afterlife, Pioneer Spirits*, and *Crystals for Healing*. She also co-wrote *Lessons of Many Lives* with hypnotherapist Melissa Watts.

As a professional writer, Karen is the author of several cookbooks and nutritional books, and she has ghost written a number of books and penned hundreds of articles about a variety of topics. She's also a published author in *Chicken Soup for the Soul: Find Your Inner Strength!* and *Chicken Soup for the Soul: Think Possible!*

Karen is a columnist for *Paranormal Underground Magazine*. She currently writes two columns for the magazine: Dream Interpretation, and Metaphysics and Energy Healing. She is also co-host of *Paranormal Underground Radio,* and she formerly served as *Paranormal Underground's* Managing Editor. Karen is also a member of Spirit Healing and Resolution (SHARe), a collective of psychic mediums and energy healers dedicated to helping people dealing with afterlife experiences and hauntings, as well as offering spiritual coaching and energy healing services.

Karen is an intuitive energy healer who is a Usui Reiki Ryoho Master/Teacher (Shinpiden) and a certified animal Usui Reiki Ryoho practitioner, as well as an ordained minister for the International Metaphysical Ministry. She has also studied numerous energy and alternative healing techniques including Quantum Touch, aromatherapy, sound healing, metaphysical healing, and crystal healing. She holds a Bachelor of Metaphysical Science (B.MSc) and a Masters of Metaphysical Science (M.MSc) from University of Metaphysics and a PhD in Metaphysical Parapsychology from the

University of Sedona. She is currently working towards her Doctor of Divinity (DD) specializing in Spiritual Healing at University of Metaphysics.

Karen is a Nia White Belt who also holds certificates in Life Coaching and Life Purpose Coaching. She teaches classes in vibrational and energy healing, Reiki, and psychic development.

AuthorKarenFrazier.com